LAND OF CHRIST

LAND

ANDRÉ PARROT

Translated by
JAMES H. FARLEY

OF CHRIST

archaeology

history

geography

FORTRESS PRESS · PHILADELPHIA

© 1968 BY FORTRESS PRESS

Library of Congress Catalog Card Number 68-15863

1-960 Printed in U.S.A. 6220J67

To the memory of
MY MOTHER AND FATHER
who in 1928
had the joy of journeying in the
LAND OF CHRIST.

Table of Contents

In Those Days ix

I. Birth and Infancy 1

II. John the Baptist and Jesus 7

III. Jesus in Galilee 18

IV. Jesus and the Samaritans 65

V. Jesus in Perea and in Judea 70

VI. Jesus at Jerusalem 77

VII. Maundy Thursday to Easter Sunday 106

VIII. Resurrection and Ascension 133

Synoptic Tables
  Table I Herodian Dynasty 143
  Table II Administration of Palestine During
            the New Testament Period 144
  Table III Chronology of the Passion 145

Selected Bibliography 147

List of Illustrations 151

Index of Scripture References 153

Index of Names and Subjects 158

In Those Days . . . .

The pages which follow constitute neither an exegetical work nor a collection of sermons. They attempt simply to situate the gospel drama in its time and place. How do we explain this excursus into the world of the New Testament? Were we called upon to justify this, we would say that, with some interruptions, we have sojourned nearly forty years in the Near East, and we have lived intimately in its heart, in its villages and in its "wilderness"; out of that experience we are able to bring a personal testimony that differs in certain respects from those which have been provided up to now. More than ever, we remain faithful to an understanding of Revelation that must be grasped in words, in acts, and especially in a person. For "the Word became flesh and dwelt among us."

What was it like "in those days"? Our intention is to attempt to give, wherever possible, a detailed description of those times. Of course, for this purpose we have called upon archaeology, which remains a marvelously rich mine of information. We have also called upon history and geography, which must not be ignored, even though their data sometimes pose problems. In some cases, there are no easy answers. But is it not better thus? And is it not time to ask again the question of the psalmist: *"What is man?"* To be sure, man today believes that he is able to embark upon the conquest of the cosmos, yet he is still incapable of crossing the threshold of life and of forbidding death to enter in. The essential escapes man, whereas all evidence indicates that Jesus was master over the whole of creation. It would be truly difficult to believe that the firsthand witnesses and the millions of later Christians — who have believed the witnesses although they themselves have not seen — have been the victims of a gigantic hoax. The record is there, at our disposal.

Four Gospels, four men, four temperaments, four vocations — the Romans have represented them abundantly and symbolically on the tympana of their cathedrals: Matthew, a man; Mark, a lion; Luke, an ox; John, an eagle. The four surround the Christ in majesty, seated on his throne, his right hand raised in blessing. His left hand holds the sacred book. It is this that we must now open.

I. Birth and Infancy

1 *Now when Jesus was born in Bethlehem of Judea in the days of Herod the King (Matthew 2:1)*

❶ There were two Bethlehems. One was in Galilee, in the territory of Zebulun (Josh. 19:15–16; Judg. 12:8). This is the present Beit Lahm, a small village with Hellenistic and Byzantine ruins. The second Bethlehem was in Judea, sometimes also called Bethlehem Ephrathah (I Chron. 4:4; Gen. 35:19; Ruth 1:2).

It is to Micah (5:2) that we owe the prophecy that was to be fulfilled. In addition, this city in which Jesus was born was also called the city of David (I Sam. 16:1).

The Herod of this passage is Herod the Great, son of the Idumean Antipater. In 37 B.C., Herod was made "king of the Jews," by favor of Rome and decision of the Senate. His kingdom covered Judea, Samaria, Galilee, and, beyond the Jordan, Perea, Galanitis, Batanea, Auranitis, Trachonitis, and a part of Iturea.

King Herod died in 4 B.C. The Gospel which places the birth of Jesus at the end of Herod's reign (Matt. 2:19) was not mistaken. The error was made by the monk Dionysius Exiguus (*ca.* A.D. 500–50) who, when he attempted to determine the Christian Era, missed by at least four years.

On the death of Herod the Great, Rome divided his kingdom according to his will.

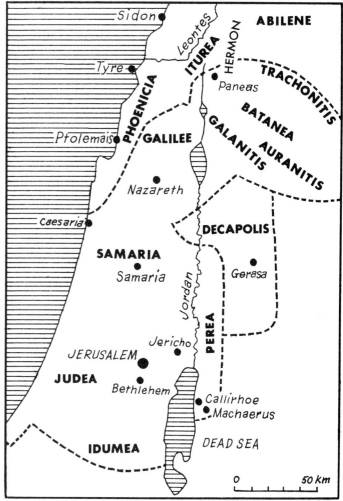

1. Palestine in the time of Herod the Great.

Herod's three sons shared in the division. Judea, Idumea, and Samaria were given to Archelaus, who received the title of ethnarch. Archelaus was deposed in A.D. 6, and was exiled to Vienne in Gaul. Thereafter, his territory was administered by procurators. Galilee and Perea were placed under the rule of Herod Antipas, who was raised to the status of tetrarch. The remainder of the territory was given to Philip, who received the same title.

❶ The wise men constituted a religious caste in Iran. According to Herodotus, this caste was of such importance that it ranked as one of the six tribes of the Medes. After the arrival of the Persians, the magi retained all of their influence. They often played a preeminent political role. The story of the magus Gaumata (6th century B.C.), who pretended to be Smerdis brought to life again and who laid claim to the crown against Cambyses, says much about the am-

2/3. The Wise Men. Virgin and Child. *Portal of Moissac.*

1 *The flight to Egypt (Matthew 2:13)*
2 *Return to Nazareth (Matthew 2:23)*
3 *In those days a decree went out from Caesar Augustus that all the world should be enrolled. . . . Quirinius was governor of Syria (Luke 2:1–2)*

bitions of the magi. Fire-worshipers, astrologers, interpreters of dreams and portents, prophets, they were as much feared as respected. Their teachings extended well beyond Iran. Twice we find mention of men who were of this school: Simon, in Samaria (Acts 8:9), and Bar-Jesus, on the island of Cyprus (Acts 13:6). It is well known how the legend grew up around the travelers who arrived at Jerusalem following "the star" (a comet, according to some scholars). On the basis of their gifts (gold, frankincense, and myrrh), it was quickly concluded that there were only three of them. They were even named: Caspar, Melchior, and Balthasar. Their representation in religious art (sculpture and painting) is so abundant that it defies cataloguing.

❶ The flight into Egypt is found only in the first Gospel. Egypt was often considered a land of refuge: Abraham, Jeroboam, the prophets Uriah and Jeremiah, the high priest Onias III, to name only a few, found asylum in the country of the Nile. At the time of Herod, Egypt was a Roman province with a very significant Jewish Diaspora.

❷ The Evangelist who makes note of the death of Herod and the accession of Archelaus explains why Nazareth was chosen: Joseph was afraid to return to Judea, which was under the jurisdiction of Archelaus. That the Romans deposed Archelaus in A.D. 6 indicates well enough that this personage was not very easy to get along with. At Nazareth, Joseph was in the territory of Herod Antipas, who was perhaps less redoubtable.

❸ Another account of the birth brings together (quite in Luke's style) two other historical personages, this time Romans. Caesar Augustus, born in 63 B.C., was the

4. The Emperor Augustus. *Museum of the Louvre.*

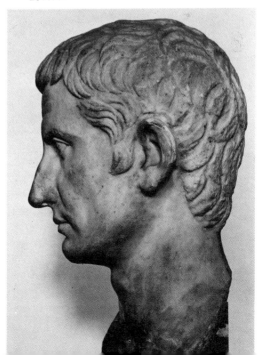

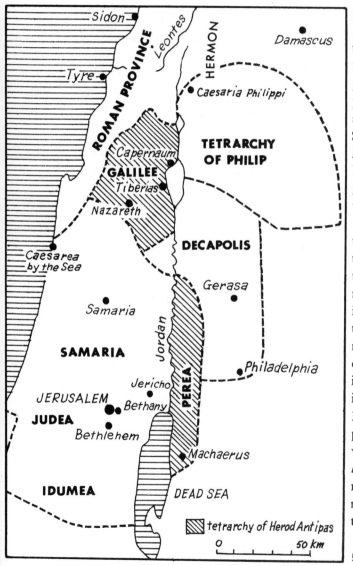

5. Palestine in the time of Jesus.

nephew and adopted son of Julius Caesar. He became emperor in 30 B.C., and received the title of Augustus, which he retained until his death in A.D. 14. Luke's notation presents major difficulties. In effect, it places the birth of Jesus during the time of a census that had been decreed by Publius Sulpicius Quirinius, when, according to Matthew, Herod the Great was still living. Now we know precisely the names of the governors of Syria during this period: Sentius Saturninus (9–6 B.C.) and Q. Varus (6–4 B.C.). As for Quirinius, he would have taken up his duties only afterwards, that is to say, *after* the birth of Jesus. According to Josephus, the census under Quirinius did not take place until A.D. 6. The chronological difference is, then, serious, and the solutions proposed to resolve this difference are not very satisfactory. For example, it is claimed that a missing name on a mutilated inscription found at Tivoli is that of Quirinius, who became governor of Syria in 3–2 B.C. and who would have been able to preside over a census whose publication would then have been made by Varus, thus *before* the death of Herod. Another theory maintains that Varus was the titular governor and Quirinius was the commander of the troops in Syria, and the latter was given the special mission of conducting the census. Many exegetes think that Luke made a mistake and antedated a census that really took place in A.D. 6, precisely under Quirinius (if one accepts the testimony of Josephus). The problem is extremely complex. However, considering the scrupulousness of Luke the physician, it is perhaps wiser to postpone the solution or the explication. One never knows but that the soil of Rome or of the East will give up some new document that may bring light which is presently lacking.

Tradition has put the birthplace in Bethlehem, in a cave. It has been established that

6/7.   Bethlehem: ▲ Cave dwellings. ▼ General view.

1 *Circumcision and presentation (Luke 2:21–24)*
2 *The boy Jesus in the temple among the teachers (Luke 2:41–52)*

8. Bethlehem. Basilica of the Nativity, exterior.

9. Central nave and iconostasis.

many inhabitants of this village did indeed live like troglodytes, with their livestock, in crevices in the cliffs. The site was venerated as early as the 2nd century, and it was in order to drive out the Christians that the emperor Hadrian installed there, in A.D. 135, the cult of Adonis - Tammuz, the Phoenician god of vegetation. In the 4th century, Constantine erected a basilica on the site. The five - aisled structure has remained intact after more than sixteen centuries. However, the choir (restored by Justinian in the 6th century A.D.) covers the sacred cave.

❶ In accordance with Jewish law, Jesus was first circumcised, on the eighth day (Lev. 12:3), then presented at the temple of Jerusalem, some 5 miles from Bethlehem. The sacrifice offered on this occasion (a pair of turtledoves or two pigeons) was that chosen by poorer people. One bird was for the burnt offering, the other for the sin offering (Lev. 12:8; Luke 2:24). Afterward, Joseph and Mary set out to return to Nazareth (Luke 2:39).

❷ It is best to say that we know next to nothing concerning the years of Jesus' childhood. We have the general statement that Mary's son "increased in wisdom and in stature, and in favor with God and man."

1 *In those days. . . . (Matthew 3:1; Mark 1:9)*

2 *In the fifteenth year of the reign of Tiberius Caesar, Pontius Pilate being governor of Judea, and Herod being tetrarch of Galilee, and his brother Philip . . . and Lysanias . . . in the high-priesthood of Annas and Caiaphas, the word of God came to John the son of Zechariah in the wilderness (Luke 3:1–2)*

The only episode that emerges from this obscure period is that in which Jesus, having come with his parents to Jerusalem for a feast of the Passover, was found by them "sitting among the teachers, listening to them and asking them questions." Christian iconography has found a great source of inspiration in this scene. As a famous example, let us mention a Russian icon from the 15th century (Wehrlin Collection), in which the child does not seem to be at all intimidated by finding himself in the presence of the venerable teachers of Israel.

The Evangelist speaks of "a day's journey" (2:44), the terminus of which has been traditionally located at el-Bireh, some 10 miles north of Jerusalem. At the end of this day's journey, Joseph and Mary could not find their son and retraced their route in search of him.

II. John the Baptist and Jesus

❶ Matthew and Mark apparently did not feel it necessary to note more carefully the moment that marked the beginning of Jesus' ministry as well as the activity of John the Baptist. The physician Luke, on the other hand, considered that history and geography were fundamental elements and that it was necessary to make them known not only to a certain Theophilus, but, after him, to his future readers as well. It is to Luke that we owe this procession which advances solemnly out of the depths of the ages.

❷ First of all, the personages, in order of importance:

Tiberius Caesar was the adopted son and

10. The Emperor Tiberius. *Museum of the Louvre.*

1 The voice of one crying in the wilderness (Matthew 3:3; Mark 1:3; Luke 3:4; John 1:23)

successor of Augustus (d. A.D. 14). The "fifteenth year" would fall in A.D. 29, according to the chronology of the monk Dionysius Exiguus (which we know to be inexact by at least four or five years).

Pontius Pilate, the Roman procurator from A.D. 26 to 36, would never have passed into posterity had it not been for the drama of Good Friday.

Herod Antipas, the son of Herod the Great and Malthace,[1] was made tetrarch of Galilee and Perea at the death of his father (4 B.C.). He was deposed in A.D. 39, at which time the emperor Caligula exiled him to St. Bertrand de Comminges in Gaul.

Philip, the son of Herod the Great and Cleopatra of Jerusalem, was tetrarch of Iturea (in the hilly country of the Anti-Lebanon) and Trachonitis (region of Bozrah, capital of Hauran), to the northeast of the Upper Jordan. At his death in A.D. 34, his territories were incorporated into the Roman province of Syria.

Lysanias was tetrarch of Abilene, the region between Hermon and Jordan. This princeling is known from two inscriptions, one of which comes from Suk Wadi Barada, the ancient Abila.

[1] For the chronology of the Herodian family, see *infra,* Table I.

Annas and Caiaphas were high priests. Caiaphas was high priest from A.D. 18 to 36. Appointed for life, he was therefore in office at the time of the events. The Annas who is mentioned in this passage was deposed in A.D. 15. He was the father-in-law of Caiaphas and retained a great deal of influence even after he ceased his official functions. This explains why he continued to be mentioned (cf. John 18:12, 24; Acts 4:6).

❶ The Four Evangelists put this phrase from the Old Testament (Isa. 40:3–5) into the mouth of John the Baptist. The phrase generally is subject to a monumental misinterpretation. Ask any ten persons who use it (for it has become a proverbial statement), and at least nine of them will probably say that it means a voice raised futilely, since no one listens to it. Thus it is said, for instance, of a preacher who speaks without receiving any response—his eloquence falls into the void.

However, *the voice of one crying in the wilderness* evokes quite another thing, even exactly the opposite. The mistake originated in a misplacing of punctuation, after which the passage was lifted out of context. Here is the text as it is found in Isaiah:

11.   John the Baptist. *Charterhouse of Pavia.*

"A voice cries: 'In the wilderness prepare the way of the Lord, make straight in the desert a highway for our God. Every valley shall be lifted up, and every mountain and hill be made low; the uneven ground shall become level, and the rough places a plain. And the glory of the Lord shall be revealed, and all flesh shall see it together, for the mouth of the Lord has spoken.' "

John the Baptist, then, likens himself to the messenger of the Old Covenant, but in order to prepare for the coming of the Lord of the New Covenant. This message which he takes up is perfectly clear and is evocative of life in the Near East—today as in former times. On two occasions, once on the Middle Euphrates and once in southern Mesopotamia, the full meaning of this "voice" was brought home to us, for the commandments of this voice were and are part of the customs of these regions. In a country where roads are rare and in some areas do not exist at all, it sometimes happens that a great personage (king or provincial governor) will decide to visit a district which lies outside of the customary circuit. The local constabulary is hastily notified and its messengers spread out to give the village or tribal chieftains the order to prepare a "road" to enable the official convoy to pass. A route is marked out and all of a sudden the whole "wilderness" is in a flutter: fellahin and Bedouins hasten, with makeshift tools, to level the bumps, fill in the ruts, and grade the ditches. In a few days a pathway is prepared in places which seemed to defy any such enterprise, and the procession is able to go through a province that was previously inaccessible to any type of Western vehicle.

It was this type of thing that was evoked by the prophet when he proclaimed the coming arrival of the God of Israel, returning from the Babylonian Exile, through the Syrian Desert. Just as one prepared the pathway for the chariots of the earthly sovereigns, so—and how much more—should one prepare the pathway of the divine monarch. This obviously is a symbolic image. Yahweh was represented by no effigy and was not to return to Palestine in a chariot, like Marduk or Nabu. This did not preclude the implication that his return must be prepared for and that the recesses and crannies of the human soul needed this straightening out.

The "voice" which cried, therefore, did not speak in the wilderness in the sense that we wrongly understand the term, for in the Near East the wilderness is never void.

12. In the wilderness.

1 *In those days came John the Baptist, preaching in the wilderness of Judea (Matthew 3:1; Mark 1:4; Luke 3:3)*

2 *His food was locusts and wild honey (Matthew 3:4; Mark 1:6)*

When one feels lost there and far from any human presence, one does not have to wait long. Slowly, men begin to appear. One had not even suspected their presence, yet their tents were not far away, hidden behind a hill, set up on the edge of a wadi. And these men run up to you, ready to help you and to offer you hospitality in their tent-houses.

It was these men of the desert, the Syrian Desert or the Judean Desert, whom Isaiah and John the Baptist summoned. And their voices proclaimed the necessity of preparing the way of the Lord of the world and the Savior of men. Each person understood that this time it was a matter not of setting off to wield the pickaxe, but of preparing his soul to receive worthily the one who was announced.

13.   Palestinian locusts.

❶   The wilderness of Judea is not an extended plain or a region covered with sand dunes. On the contrary, it is a mountainous region, cut by deep valleys and extending eastward on a line from Jerusalem to Hebron. Today it is roamed by nomadic mountain tribes such as the Taᶜamireh. The region has been made famous by the discovery of the "Dead Sea Scrolls." The only settled inhabitants are the Greek monks of the monasteries of Koziba or of Mar Sabas.

❷   We have eaten some excellent honey at Jericho. Was it "wild"? We do not know. The locusts are enormous grasshoppers, the plague of the East, the deadly enemy of the vineyards. They move in enormous clouds and greatly damage crops when they alight. They are said to be edible. On this point, we shall have to be excused from bearing personal testimony. . . .

11

1 *John wore a garment of camel's hair, and a leather girdle around his waist (Matthew 3:4)*

2 *They were baptized by him in the river Jordan (Matthew 3:5–6)*

3 *This took place in Bethany beyond the Jordan, where John was baptizing (John 1:28)*

4 *Brood of vipers (Matthew 3:7; Luke 3:7)*

❶ One is on the wrong track when one pictures John the Baptist half-naked, bare-headed, with a simple loincloth around his waist. This wild Palestinian probably wore, besides his cloth tunic, a cloak made of camel's hair. Even today, the *abayeh* of camel's hair is more expensive and less common than coats of goat's hair or lamb's wool. The leather girdle is rather large, permitting one to enclose one's valuables inside it (Matt. 10:9). Often a dagger was also slipped into the belt.

❷ John appeared in the region beyond the Jordan, in a dreary and drab land. The Jordan cuts a passage through chalky soil, and is bordered by thick groves of tamarisk trees.

14. A pair of sandals.

❸ Bethany beyond the Jordan is to be distinguished from the village of Lazarus. The location is unknown. Origen has corrected it to Bethabara, but the Johannine text is to be preferred. This Bethany is also different from the place of Jesus' baptism, which is further to the south, east of Jericho and on the right bank of the river. Another passage in John (3:23) gives a different topographical indication: Aenon near Salim. These places are unknown and are almost impossible to localize. Moreover, it is not certain that these places should be sought on the banks of the Jordan. John also preached as he baptized, and this preaching was not always tender to the ears of those who heard it.

❹ Of all the venomous animals, the viper is undoubtedly the most fearsome. The small, sable-colored horned viper attacks only when it is disturbed. Its bite is fatal.

12

1   *The thong of whose sandals I am not worthy to stoop down and untie (Mark 1:7 and parallels). Whose sandals I am not worthy to carry (Matthew 3:11)*

2   *Jesus came from Nazareth of Galilee and was baptized by John in the Jordan (Mark 1:9; Matthew 3:13; Luke 3:21)*

1 The common footwear was the sandal, with thongs to secure the feet. In order to remove the sandals of someone who wished to relax, it was necessary to kneel before him and untie the thongs. However, often one preferred to walk barefoot, in order to travel more swiftly. This explains the passage in Matthew: John the Baptist is compared to a servant who *carries* the sandals of his master, who naturally preceded him on the route.

2 The site of the baptism of Jesus has not been located with any precision, except by traditions going back to the 3rd century A.D. It is pointed out on the right bank of the river, more or less opposite Jericho, not far from a Greek monastery dedicated to its memory, today called Qasr el-Yehud.

Even today, in the dead of winter, on the night of Epiphany, the Greek Orthodox of Jerusalem and its environs go there to perform baptisms. On January 19, 1928 we witnessed this ceremony, which has a certain grandeur. During the evening, encampments were set up on the banks of the river; here the families waited patiently, gathered

15.   The Jordan in Upper Galilee.

quet of green foliage in the water, he ritually sprinkled the guests in the boats and the faithful who were standing or kneeling on the bank. Suddenly, just before the rising of the sun, men and women literally surged out from all the campfires. They were wearing long white robes (which, we were told, would later serve as shrouds). They ran to the river, and, with fervor and no small degree of heroism, they plunged into the glacial waters. It was a rapidly accomplished "in-and-out," and those who remained on the steep river banks hastily brought clothing heated over the flames of the fires. They also brought a boiling tea to the shivering arrivals.

16. Greek Orthodox women on the banks of the Jordan.

around fires fed, after a fashion, with freshly cut stems and branches which gave off more smoke than heat. The Archbishop of Philadelphia had officiated first, around 4 A.M., in a tent promoted to the rank of sanctuary. As dawn began to break, the crosiered and mitered prelate, escorted by deacons, got into a small boat. He was followed by his guests, consular representatives. A whole procession formed on the water. Several times the archbishop traced long signs of the cross in the swiftly flowing water. Then, after having dipped a bou-

Meanwhile, a real baptism was being prepared: a naked little infant was taken out of a coverlet. The priest rolled up his sleeves, and abruptly two shaggy arms took hold of this poor, frail flesh and plunged it into a tub of lukewarm water three times, in the name of the Father, and of the Son, and of the Holy Spirit. The little newly baptized one cried a lot, we'll have to say that. Still, it was a great privilege to be baptized on the night of the Epiphany, on the banks of the Jordan, with water from the Jordan, at the site of Jesus' baptism.

1 *And he was in the wilderness forty days, tempted by Satan (Mark 1:13; Matthew 4:1–2; Luke 4:2)*

2 *Command these stones to become loaves of bread (Matthew 4:3)*

3 *All the kingdoms of the world and the glory of them (Matthew 4:8)*

❶ The episode of the Temptation was also located "in the wilderness," where Jesus stayed for "forty days." As for John the Baptist, the "wilderness" was the desolate country west or southwest of Jericho. Some scholars have advanced the thesis that the precursor as well as he whom he came to baptize had spent some time at Qumran, among the Essenes. Nothing in the texts permits us to suppose this.

As is well known, the story of the Temptation is highlighted by three scenes in which Satan intervenes: the stones, the kingdoms, the temple.

❷ In Palestine, especially in the wilderness of Judea, these words are thrown into bold relief. Not a tree, not a tuft of grass. Nothing but stones. In order for a man lost in this wilderness not to die of hunger, it would be absolutely necessary for these stones to be changed into bread.

❸ Tradition has located the place of Jesus' withdrawal at Jebel Qarantal, a precipitous cliff which overlooks Jericho from a height of over 1600 feet. Ptolemy, the son-in-law of Simon Maccabeus, had a fort there which was the scene of several assassi-

17. The Mountain of the Temptation—Jebel Qarantal.

1 *The devil . . . set him on the pinnacle of the temple, and said to him, ". . . throw yourself down" (Matthew 4:6)*

nations. It was replaced in the 4th century A.D. by a church dedicated to the memory of the Temptation. Today a monastery of Greek monks (Sarandarion) is perched halfway up the steep cliff. These poor, bearded monks, in rags and tatters, welcome cordially anyone who ascends to their monastery. They live far from the world, in the rocks, looking out over a grandiose panorama: below them, the "city of palms" in its oasis, the steppe, then the line of the Jordan which one can make out by the coppices bordering it (such are the trees "planted by streams of water" of Ps. 1:3). Finally, in the background, the extraordinary range of the mountains of Moab which, in the evening, at sunset, take on hues of mauve and violet such as we have seen nowhere else. If Jesus was in this "wilderness," this is what lay beneath him and this is what he contemplated with his eyes. Some thirteen centuries before, but on the other side of the Jordan, from Mount Nebo, Moses had viewed the inverse of this same panorama.

❶ One hesitates to attempt to locate the "height" or, as it is sometimes translated, the "pinnacle" of the temple. With many authors, we feel that it should be located at the southeast corner of the present Haram.

◀ 18.   The pinnacle of the temple.

1 He was with the wild beasts (Mark 1:13)
2 Herod . . . shut up John in prison (Luke 3:19–20)

The wall that one sees today was built on Herodian foundations, the foundations of the sanctuary of Jesus' day. It rises some 55 feet over the present ground level, but under the rubbish and debris, its base was not reached for more than 140 feet. (By comparison, the Arc de Triomphe de l'Etoile is 160 feet high.) To throw oneself down would obviously mean death by crushing on the rocks. This was, in fact, the place where James the brother of Jesus was martyred (A.D. 62).

❶ By considering the fauna of Palestine today (less varied than that of Biblical times), we can easily give some names: jackals, hyenas, foxes, wolves, wildcats, even leopards and cheetahs. From time to time there were undoubtedly lions also. The "lion of Bashan" and those which attacked the flocks (Amos 3:12) existed well beyond the time of Christ and into the Middle Ages. There are innumerable clay tablets upon which the ancients have represented the royal animal, and there are also some stone reliefs, such as the slab of Beisan, the lion of Sheik Saad. We should also add vipers, snakes which hid among the rocks, and eagles, vultures which nested in the crags of the cliffs.

❷ The arrest of John the Baptist came shortly after the baptism of Jesus. John had clearly censured the behavior of Herod Antipas, who lived with Herodias, the wife of his brother Philip (Mark 6:17–19).[1] None of the Evangelists gives any details about the place of imprisonment. However, we know from the Jewish historian Josephus that John was imprisoned at Machaerus. Herod the Great had built a palace-fortress there, above Callirhoe, whose waters were renowned. His son Herod Antipas, tetrarch of Perea, inherited it. The fortress, which overlooked the Dead Sea (eastern shore) was isolated enough, and it is easy to understand how this residence could be a favorite of the kinglet, who conducted his illicit love affairs there. This did not prevent him from advertising them publicly on occasion.

19.   Lion of Sheik Saad (Karnaim).

[1] Instead of Philip, some scholars propose another Herod, who also would have been a son of Herod the Great.

III. Jesus in Galilee

1 *Jesus in Galilee*

His birthday, for example, was a good excuse to have a banquet and dancing—and the execution of the Forerunner (Mark 6: 21–29; Matt. 14:3–12).

No one knows what became of the body of the Baptist. It seems that it was given to his disciples (Mark 6:29; Matt. 14:12), who buried it. A "tomb" is mentioned, but no details are given concerning its location. Was it at Machaerus itself? Or was the body transported as far as Samaria? In Samaria, a Crusaders church (built over a 4th-century basilica) is consecrated to the Baptist, and his sepulcher is venerated there. The Baptist's head had a fate as eventful as uncertain: it was supposedly carried from Palestine to Cilicia, then to Constantinople, although today it is the object of veneration at Damascus, in the mosque of the Omayyads! It is better to confess that we are sure of nothing about this.

1 The Synoptics and the Fourth Gospel have different traditions regarding Jesus' Galilean ministry. John also has certain events and acts that the others do not have. For example, John indicates that the Galilean ministry was not continuous, but was interrupted by several trips to Jerusalem. To enter into these problems of exegesis would lead us away from our essential purpose, which is primarily to replace the facts in their framework. This statement will become clearer, since we will follow here a purely geographical rather than chronological approach.

2 During the time of Jesus, Galilee was under the control of Herod Antipas. Galilee is in the north of Palestine; its northern border touches Phoenicia, that is to say, "the district of Tyre and Sidon" (Matt. 15:21; Mark 7:31); the Mediterranean is on

2 *Now when he heard that John had been arrested, he withdrew into Galilee; and leaving Nazareth he went and dwelt in Capernaum (Matthew 4:12–13; Mark 1:14; Luke 4:14; John 4:43 and 2:12)*

◄ 20. Tiberias.

21. Magdala—Mejdel.

22. General view of Nazareth.

23. Sea of Galilee (view from the north).
24. Plain of Gennesaret.
▼

25. Region of the Sea of Galilee.

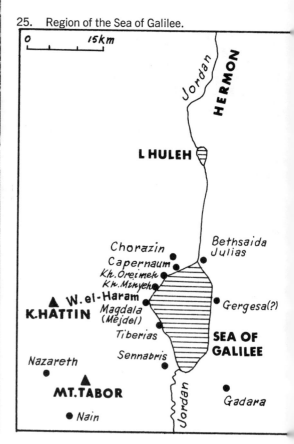

20

the west; to the east is the Jordan; to the south of the Plain of Esdraelon lies Samaria. The capital of Galilee was Tiberias, a city founded by Herod Antipas between A.D. 17 and 22; he so named it in order to flatter the vanity of the Roman suzerain, the em-

26. The Jordan River at the Bridge of Jacob's Daughters.

peror Tiberius. Endowed with a stadium and a forum, it had all the features of a Hellenistic city. Despite its synagogues, it does not seem that Jesus ever stopped there. At least the Gospels have retained no memory of this. Other cities played a more important part: Nazareth, where Jesus spent his childhood (Luke 2:39), some 20 miles west of Tiberias and the large towns on the shores of the lake; Magdala (today Mejdel), the city from which Mary Magdalene came (Luke 8:2 [NEB]), about 3 miles north of Tiberias; and especially Capernaum (today Tell Hum).

❶ The sea was the Sea of Galilee (Mark 1:16), also called the Sea of Tiberias (John 6:1; 21:1). The oldest name had been the Sea of Chinnereth (Num. 34:11; Josh. 13:27), from the name of a locality on the lakeshore (today Khan Oreimeh). One also finds it called the Lake of Gennesaret (Luke 5:1), from the rich plain on its northwest shore. The lake is a sheet of water about 13 miles long and 7 miles wide, lying 682 feet below sea level. Such are the cold statistics. What these figures do not tell is the unique, unforgettable impression the lake makes on someone seeing it for the first time. When one comes from Nazareth, there all at once is the lake, calm and blue.

21

1 *And passing along by the Sea of Galilee, he saw Simon and Andrew the brother of Simon casting a net in the sea; for they were fishermen (Mark 1:16; Matthew 4:18)*

If one approaches from Semakh, one comes upon the lake without expecting it and without having any time to prepare oneself for this great pool of water. If, on the contrary, one descends from the Anti-Lebanon, after the Bridge of Jacob's Daughters, one receives a completely different impression. There is the lake, at midday, at the bottom of a great basin, and as one descends it seems always larger, farther off, more majestic. A preparation, an adjustment, is necessary for this encounter. It is something long desired, awaited, and yet it is too soon arrived, the fulfillment, the accomplishment of the dream: to walk along the shores of the Sea of Galilee, to see it with one's own eyes, to dip one's hands into its waters, to peer across the lake for the sight of a fishing boat. There are no longer many boats,

and rare are the sails. Thirty years ago Father Abel counted twenty-six of them!

Yet one sail suffices; with this one alone the whole gospel history comes back: the calling and the summons of the first disciples (Mark 1:17); the storm abated (Mark 4:37–41; Matt. 8:23–27; Luke 8:22–25); the miraculous catch of fish (Luke 5:4–11; John 21:2–8). The "Galilean idyll" . . . why not? The scenery is too grand here, nature is too welcoming, with its meadows full of red and yellow waves of myriad flowers, anemones and daisies, when in spring life smiles at the sun.

❶ Navigation and fishing were the resources provided by the Sea. Both, during the Roman era, were extremely flourishing. The Gospels contain many references to the

27. Fishing boats on the Sea of Galilee.

28. A restless Sea of Galilee. ▶

comings and goings between the shores of the lake (Matt. 8:28; 9:1; 14:13, 22, 34; 15:39; 16:5; Mark 4:35; 5:1, 21; 6:32, 45, 53; 8:10, 13; Luke 8:22, 26, 37; 9:10; John 6:1). When it was calm, the crossings were easy. Sometimes, however, the crossings became more difficult and even perilous. This is not to be wondered at, no matter how tranquil the water may appear. During a storm or high wind, the lake becomes agitated, and choppy waves put the small boats to a severe test. Nothing can be done but to strike sail and try to make it to land by rowing.

After navigation came fishing, a quite natural occupation along the shores of a lake that even today is full of fish and in a time when fish were an important part of the alimentation (cf. Mark 6:38; Luke 5:5). One went into partnership with others, either of the same family (Simon and his brother Andrew; James and his brother John—Mark 1:16, 19), or with hired servants (Mark 1:20), in order to charter a boat and "cast the net." The net was apparently a large, circular, weighted net which one cast either from the shore or by advancing a short distance into the water. Later it was drawn back up onto the bank. Another system consisted of letting down the net between two boats (Luke 5:7), the fish being caught in the mesh. But it was always a real task, one that was the same the world over. The net was made of very thin threads and consequently was very fragile. It was necessary to repair the breaks constantly. Such repair work was done during the daytime, whereas frequently the fishing took place at night (Luke 5:5). The sons of Zebedee were mending their nets when Jesus passed by. The first disciples were taken from among such fishermen.

1 *As Jesus passed on from there, he saw a man called Matthew sitting at the tax office; and he said to him, "Follow me." And he rose and followed him (Matthew 9:9; Mark 2:14; Luke 5:27)*

2 *Jesus . . . found Philip and said to him, "Follow me." Now Philip was from Bethsaida, the city of Andrew and Peter (John 1:43)*

❶ After the fishermen, the call was addressed to a publican (or tax collector). The scene still is set by the lakeside, but at or near Capernaum. Here one is at the frontier of the territories of Herod Antipas and Philip, and merchandise cannot move from one region to the other unless a tax is paid. What is involved, then, is a customs bureau with a collector, this Matthew whom two Gospels know as "Levi, the son of Alphaeus."

The publicans had a bad reputation, not only because they were customs officials, but also because they were given the task of collecting the taxes of the government. Consequently, they were assessed a certain sum, which spurred them to squeeze the taxpayers well beyond what was really owed, since the overpayment was the tax collector's gain. It is understandable why these officials were universally spurned and why they were purely and simply included in the category of "sinners" (Matt. 9:11; Mark 2:15; Luke 5:30). In choosing one of his disciples from this social class, Jesus was not afraid to shock those who saw it nor, even at the outset, to render justice to those individuals who had not quite deserved such infamy.

Moreover, the task of the tax collector was not an easy one. Honest men, in order to collect the customs taxes, had to apply very complicated regulations. An example of such regulations is found in the "tariff of Palmyra," written in Greek and Palmyrene, promulgated by the senate of that city (A.D. 137). This document fixes the tariffs due, and covers hundreds of cases.

But for each honest man, how many doubtful characters there were, how many who were not able to resist the temptation! Such was Zacchaeus himself, the chief tax collector of Jericho (Luke 19:2) and very rich (undoubtedly from his tax-collecting practices). After his encounter with Jesus, Zacchaeus took the initiative of "restoring fourfold" (Luke 19:8) to those whom he had defrauded!

❷ With Philip, we have a new call and a new obedience. Bethsaida, to the east of the "Little Jordan," had been founded shortly before the Christian Era by the tetrarch Philip. It was called Julias in honor of the daughter of the Emperor Augustus. The site should be sought at the place today called et-Tell, a short distance from the shore. An attentive reading of the texts (Mark 6:45; Luke 9:10) will show that it is in no wise implied that the city bordered on the lake.

24

1 *He entered the synagogue and taught (Luke 6:6)*

2 *And he came to Nazareth, where he had been brought up; and he went to the synagogue, as his custom was, on the sabbath day. And he stood up to read; and there was given to him the book of the prophet Isaiah (Luke 4:16–17)*

Of the twelve apostles, five are without doubt Galileans: Simon, Andrew, James, John, Philip. The sixth, Matthew, since he was a government official, could have come from another province, having been assigned to the customs office at Capernaum by the needs of the service. Of the others, we have only their names: Bartholomew, Thomas, James the son of Alphaeus, Thaddaeus (=Lebbaeus=Judas the son of James), Simon the Zealot, and Judas Iscariot. The sobriquet "Iscariot" does not mean, as has been believed, "from Kerioth," but, according to the ingenious hypothesis of Harald Ingholt, "a man of ruddy complexion."

❶ The Gospels agree in reporting that Jesus readily addressed his teaching to those who gathered together in the synagogues each sabbath. Thus, without having to call them together, he found a group of hearers ready to listen, if not always ready to approve (Luke 4:28–29).

❷ There is no doubt about the location of Nazareth—the identification with the en-Nasirah of our time has never raised the slightest difficulty. What is curious, however, is that Nazareth is not mentioned at all in the Old Testament, in Josephus, or in the Talmud. It was at Nazareth that Jesus

29. The Apostles John and Peter. *Arles, Portal of St. Trophime.*

spent his childhood, his "hidden years," in a family where he himself followed the trade of carpenter (Mark 6:3; Matt. 13:55), which he perhaps took over from Joseph. It should be recalled that Paul was a tentmaker (Acts 18:3) and that some of the great rabbis also had a trade: Hillel was a

25

wood-sculptor, Shammai was a carpenter. We do not know why Nazareth was not held in higher esteem (John 1:46). Perhaps it was because of its insignificance, perhaps also because of the bad character of its inhabitants. The latter, it seems, were never won over to the side of their compatriot (Matt. 13:54–58), who was severe with them (vs. 57).

The site of the synagogue of Nazareth has never been rediscovered – which does not hinder natives from showing it to pilgrims and tourists! On the other hand, the Franciscan Custodian of the Holy Land is in the process of erecting on the ruins of the Church of the Crusaders (itself built on a Byzantine sanctuary) an enormous basilica dedicated to the memory of the Annunciation. The church, it is said, will be able to shelter six thousand of the faithful.

The worship service in the synagogue contained a reading by an assistant, who stood as he read. This came after the prayer and before the sermon. The Law was read first, then the Prophets. The scripture was read in Hebrew, but immediately translated into Aramaic, the language of the times. Each of the books of the Old Testament formed a scroll, which was more or less unrolled until the assistant came to the text that he

30. The Scroll of Isaiah, from Qumran.

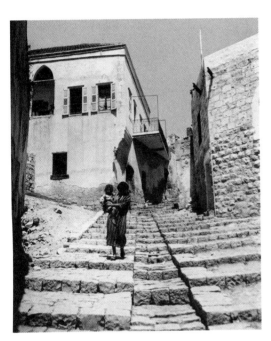

31. A street in Nazareth.

32. Mountain of the Precipitation.

desired to read (the choice was his). After the reading was finished and the scroll was returned to the servant, the same person could give his commentary on the text. It seems that Jesus had followed this procedure (Luke 4:21). These scrolls, which were made of parchment, papyrus, or leather, were then placed in a special cabinet or in a chest in the interior of the synagogue. We could wish for no better illustration of these practices than certain of the Dead Sea Scrolls, particularly the Scroll of Isaiah (Qumran Cave 1): it is made of seventeen pieces of leather, sewn end to end, and the entire scroll is approximately 290 inches long and 10 inches high.

The scene at Nazareth ends in a tumult. Jesus' compatriots put him out of the city and led him to the brow of the hill on which the city was built. There they tried to throw him down headlong (Luke 4:29–

30). The region of the Precipitation has not been located with any precision, although it is shown nevertheless at Jebel Qafzeh (about 2 miles south of Nazareth). This seems a bit far, and it is improbable that the houses had advanced that distance. On the other hand, no ruins exist on the plateau of Nebi-Sahin that overlooks the city. Consequently, every attempt to locate the site seems untenable. Indeed, of all the "holy places" in Nazareth (today in the Israeli zone), not one is certain. Only the spring, called the Fountain of the Virgin, could have witnessed one of the members of the holy family coming there to draw water.

The inhabitants of Nazareth could gaze upon an extensive panorama bordered on the east by the mountains of Moab, on the south — beyond the Plain of Esdraelon — by the hills of Samaria, on the west by the mountain range of Carmel. Thus we can understand perfectly how the memory of Elijah and Elisha could be recalled to them (Luke 4:25–27).

1 There were two towns named Cana. One was in Phoenicia, some 6 miles southeast of Tyre. The other was "in Galilee," as the text makes explicit. This Cana should be sought at Kefr Kenna, 6 miles from Nazareth in the direction of Tiberias. Sev-

33. General view of Cana.

1 *And they went into Capernaum and immediately on the sabbath he entered the synagogue and taught (Mark 1:21; Luke 4:31)*

eral churches vie for the honor of commemorating the memory of the miracle, if not its actual site. The water changed into wine was contained in the "stone jars" (vs. 6) instead of the traditional earthen jars. The Museum of the Louvre owns a container called "Vase of Cana,"[1] in white stone.

1 From Nazareth (1253 feet above sea level) to Capernaum (682 feet below sea level) one descends to the lake, as Luke has carefully noted, a descent of over 1900 feet in about 20 miles. Capernaum (or Capharnaum) was truly the center of Jesus' Galilean ministry. At the frontier between the territories of Herod Antipas and Philip, it had, as we have seen, a customs station (Matt. 9:9) and a military detachment commanded by a centurion (Luke 7:2). Thus it was a border city, well fortified by the mandatory powers. It also had a synagogue which Jesus often entered in order to teach (Mark 1:21; John 6:59). There seems to be little against the identification of Capernaum with Tell Hum, which is to be preferred over Khan Minyeh (southwest of Khan Oreimeh). Excavations begun in

34. Capernaum. The ruins of the synagogue.
35. Colonnade of the synagogue.

1866 by Wilson were undertaken in 1905 by the Germans Kohl and Watzinger, and continued in 1922 by the Franciscan fathers. At Tell Hum, Father Orfali uncovered a three-naved synagogue (80 ft. by 61 ft.)

[1] *AO*, 5026. Height: 27.3 inches. According to one tradition, it was brought to France by Saint Louis, but there is nothing to support this.

29

with a portico, partially open to the sky. This building belongs to a group called the "Palestinian synagogues" (Kerazeh, Umm el-Amed, Meron, Kefr Birim, etc.) and its decoration is related to that which was current during the time of the Severans (2nd–3rd centuries A.D.). Thus it cannot be seen as the synagogue built with the aid of the centurion (Luke 7:5). At the most, one could imagine that the synagogue uncovered in our day was erected on the site of that which Jesus saw.

Two columns were inscribed. On one, an Aramaic inscription reads: "Alphaeus, son of Zebida, son of Johanan, has made this column. Let it be for him a blessing!" On the other, written in Greek: "Herod, son of Mokimos, and Justos, his son, with their children, have raised this column." A section of the frieze on the north wall represents a sort of *naos* mounted on wheels. Perhaps this has something to do with the *merkaba* [chariot], which, according to I Chronicles (28:18), served to transport the ark, or perhaps it represents the deluxe vehicle of the Jewish patriarch. Besides the floral friezes, the ornamentation also includes marine shells, pomegranates, the Star of David, a six-lobed disk, all elements which attest to the later epoch.

36. Capernaum. The synagogue after the excavation.

37. Ornamentation of an entablature.

decorated with Corinthian columns, preceded by a terrace accessible by two staircases, and flanked on the east by a court

1 *Simon's mother-in-law lay sick with a fever (Mark 1:30; Matthew 8:14; Luke 4:38)*

2 *That evening, at sundown (Mark 1:32; Matthew 8:16; Luke 4:40)*

The corrupt city received the new preaching poorly, despite all the efforts which Jesus made, and thus it incurred the maledictions (Matt. 11:23; Luke 10:15). Judging by the documentation before 1905, Tell Hum seems to have been leveled to the ground; it is probable that this being "brought down to Hades" was due to an earthquake sometime after the 4th century A.D.

The same disastrous fate awaited two neighboring towns, Bethsaida (which we have identified above with Julias) and Chorazin (Kerazeh). Chorazin, which lies about two miles north of the lake, was also the site of the discovery of synagogue ruins. Excavations at the site were resumed in 1962. The ingratitude of these cities was all the more marked since all three rejected a message that undoubtedly would have been better received by the two great Phoenician ports, Tyre and Sidon (Luke 10:13–14).

In the light of the accounts, it appears that Galilee was a region of relatively dense population and that each important town had its own synagogue (Matt. 4:23; Mark 1:39; Luke 4:44). It was a population perhaps more formalist than religious, yet nonetheless "ready." The people were open to excitements and enthusiasms, sometimes arriving in crowds (Matt. 12:15; Mark 3:7; Luke 6:17; 8:19, etc.), avid to hear this preaching that was so clear and at the same time so profound, a message that the simplest person could understand (cf. John 7:46). They also hastened up with all the sickness and suffering that is the lot of each and every person. The physician of souls was at the same time the healer of bodies.

1 Fever and paludism [malaria] were quite frequent, even in recent times, in the plains of Hauran as well as near the lake. Here, at the bottom of the basin, a stifling and debilitating atmosphere prevails throughout the year, with the exception of a few brief weeks in winter. In this unhealthy climate, there seems to have been wisdom in the intensive cultivation of eucalyptus and in the generalized use of products of therapeutic chemistry.

2 The precise detail that is found only in Mark would seem superfluous to a Westerner. Yet it is quite a part of the Eastern spirit, for whom sundown (that is, the sun's disappearance) marks the decisive instant of the day's end. A Muslim, during the month of Ramadan, must fast during the day and may eat only at sundown. Therefore, when the sky is overcast and night is falling, he inquires very carefully about this detail: has

1 *And in the morning, a great while before day, he rose and went out to a lonely place (Mark 1:35)*

2 *And he said to them, "Let us go on to the next towns" (Mark 1:38)*

the sun disappeared from the horizon? If so, he can eat. If not, he waits until he is absolutely certain not to transgress the Koranic prescription. The Jews of Capernaum also were concerned not to break the sabbath laws.

But it was not only a question of the sabbath commandment. The people of Capernaum did not come out only to witness miracles, but because the basin, overheated during the day, would finally get a breath of fresh, cool air. The sluggish life would, suddenly and briefly, experience a renewal of activity.

❶ Well before sunrise, Jesus could easily find a secluded place: the hill is steep and one can find immediate solitude at the very gates of a city without "suburbs," like Capernaum. We learn that Jesus, who had need of meditation, arose long before day, even before dawn. In the Orient, formerly as well as today, life awakens at dawn, and then immediately the city is full of noise, uproar, hubbub. Obviously, then it was not the noise of cars and motorized vehicles, but the bleating of flocks of sheep, the raucous cry of the camels being saddled, the braying of asses being loaded, the crowing of the cocks . . . and then the women,

who already were on the way to the fountain or the well, the grain being crushed by the mill, the cakes of bread that were put on the hot oven. How could one succeed then in becoming silent within oneself?

❷ Few of these small towns remain today; at least, few existed before the installation of Zionist colonies. Bethsaida, Chorazin, Capernaum, Magdala — heaps of stone buried under brambles or under mud hamlets. Nothing remains of that garland of towns, the glory of the country.

38. Palmyra. Relief of "The Banquet."

39. Bedouin meal. ▶

32

1 *They removed the roof above him; and when they had made an opening, they let down the pallet on which the paralytic lay (Mark 2:4; Luke 5:19)*

2 *And as he sat at table in his house (Mark 2:15)*

3 *Many tax collectors and sinners were sitting with Jesus (Mark 2:15; Matthew 9:10; Luke 5:29)*

❶ Jesus has returned to Capernaum. The crowd surrounds the house that he has entered, and there is a paralytic to be healed. Those who have brought the paralytic waste no time. What they have to do is not very complicated. The terrace-roofs are easily accessible by an outside staircase that comes up from the courtyard. The cover is made of mud mixed with cut straw, which is then spread on matting supported by beams. It is not very difficult to penetrate such a roof, nor is it difficult for the mattress or litter on which the paralytic lies to be lowered into the room where Jesus is. And the healed man can easily carry his "bed" (Mark 2:12; Luke 5:24) by rolling it up under his arm or by placing it on his head.

❷ The house was either that of Simon or that of Levi (the text is not clear on this point). The Greek term translated "sat at table" should be translated: "And as Jesus *reclined* in his house. . . ." The verb is synonymous with "putting oneself at table" since one reclined while eating. This mode was in existence as early as the 8th century B.C. since Amos (6:4) mentions it (and censures it vigorously). In Jesus' day, one supported himself on his left elbow, with the head and shoulders erect. The best illustration of this position is in the funerary reliefs from Palmyra: the deceased persons are stretched out on the beds, taking their meals which have been brought to them by those left behind. We should also mention the celebrated relief discovered by Loftus at Nineveh: here one sees King Ashurbanipal, just returned from an expedition, banqueting under a vine-arbor. Today this mode has disappeared. Generally one eats seated, or better, crouched, around the platter of food which is placed upon the ground; with the right hand, one draws morsels out of the pile of food.

❸ It is not difficult to explain the presence of publicans, tax collectors, and customs officials, since Levi was one of their own. In the Orient, "guilds" are always formed from very homogeneous groups and have an active community life. As we have already pointed out in regard to the vocation of Matthew (Levi), the publicans had a bad reputation among the Jews. The "sinners" with whom they associated were people who were suspect because they did not observe the ritual prescriptions. Both types sought out Jesus (we are told that they were many), and Jesus had no fear of compromising himself by mixing with them, just as he had no fear later on of compromising himself by associating with Samaritans.

1 Now John's disciples and the Pharisees were fasting (Mark 2:18; Matthew 9:14; Luke 5:33)

His behavior caused a scandal, which was soon made manifest by the interference of the "scribes of the Pharisees" (Mark 2:16). The scribes had become a preponderant class among the Jewish people. They were the preeminent doctors and guardians of the Law. As jurists, legislators, judges, and educators, they enjoyed a great prestige. The Pharisees constituted a party whose official origins went back to the Seleucid period (2nd century B.C.), when Hellenism threatened to engulf Judaism. A strict, orthodox sect, it set itself up as the official defender of the beleaguered Law. It is easy to understand why a large number of the scribes had attached themselves to this party. Some of them, however, had joined the party of the Sadducees. In this passage, the interlocuters of the disciples are explicitly defined: they are the scribes, members of the Pharisean party.

40. "Old wineskins."

❶ Only one fast was obligatory in Israel, that of the Day of Atonement (Lev. 16:29). It is difficult to believe that Jesus, who had come "to fulfill the law," should have been in violation on this point. It was probably a question of the supplementary fast days, which were observed by the strict Pharisees. According to Luke (18:12), these fast days were observed twice weekly, on Monday and Thursday. These were optional fasts but were also recognized by the Baptist's disciples, who were of the more austere school of thought. In Matthew (6:16), Jesus did not prohibit fasting. He merely criticized the ostentatious customs of those who practiced fasting, and he indicated the proper way to fast. But in the passage under consideration, Jesus explains to those who questioned him (the scribes?) why his disciples did not fast. Jesus compares himself to a bridegroom and his disciples to the "bridegroom's friends" (NEB). It is quite evident that the latter could not consider assuming an attitude of contrition as long as the bridegroom was present.

34

1 *Old garments and new wine (Matthew 9:16–17; Mark 2:21–22; Luke 5:36–39)*

2 *One sabbath he was going through the grainfields; and as they made their way his disciples began to pluck ears of grain (Mark 2:23–28; Matthew 12:1–8; Luke 6:1–5)*

3 *The Pharisees . . . held counsel with the Herodians against him, how to destroy him (Mark 3:6)*

❶ The patching of old garments is perhaps more frequent among us than it was in Palestine during the time of Jesus. There they preferred to use the garment until it was threadbare. There was a risk involved in adding a new piece to an old garment: at the first washing of the patched garment, the new piece might shrink more than the older part, and would almost certainly cause a tear.

New wine, during the process of fermentation, put the receptacle containing it to something of a test. The container was not a cask; it was a leather skin or a jug,coated with pitch. The old wineskins were less sound, worn as they were by being transported and handled. Thus, with new wine, it was better to use new wineskins.

Once again, Jesus' teaching makes use of examples taken from the very surroundings in which he spoke. In this case, the teaching seems clear: one cannot bring about the new by utilizing the old. And more particularly: the gospel cannot be couched in an old framework.

❷ Some exegetes have thought that Jesus and his disciples, in order to clear a path, had plucked off the ears of grain that barred their way. It was simpler than that.

When one has lived in the Orient, one understands what is involved in this passage. Frequently it happens that Arabs, in order to take a shortcut, cross a planted field without hesitation. Sometimes the path follows a trail that had been utilized frequently when the land lay fallow. It provides a way of less resistance and has become a habit with the local people, which is quite normal. Thus a narrow trail is maintained in the middle of the crops. When, as in this passage, the harvest is near (in May), those who take the path are amid the stalks of grain. It is very difficult not to pluck some grains unconsciously. One would truly have to be a Pharisee to compare this with the action of harvesting, which was forbidden on the sabbath (Exod. 34:21).

❸ The episodes of the plucking of the grain and of the healing of the man with a withered hand deal with the strict observance or with the nonobservance of the sabbath. The Evangelist has grouped them together, although they perhaps did not take place on the same day. In any event, they crystallized, then hardened the opposition to Jesus: first the scribes, then the Pharisees, and now the "Herodians." The Herodians were not a sect or a political party, but were retainers of the court of

35

1 *A great multitude from Galilee followed; also from Judea and Jerusalem and Idumea and from beyond the Jordan and from about Tyre and Sidon (Mark 3:7-8)*

2 *The Sermon on the Mount*

the tetrarch, Herod Antipas. Since all of the events reported here took place in Herod's territory, it was necessary to have the support of the "powers that be" in order to reinforce the resistance to Jesus. Herod Antipas had already imprisoned John the Baptist. It was not impossible that one day, better informed, he could do the same with Jesus.

❶ This enumeration of regions indicates the success of the Galilean ministry: we have here the repercussion of the healings performed and the reverberations of the initial preaching. In effect, it was not only Galilee that was reached, but the whole territory of Herod Antipas, for "beyond the Jordan" implies Perea as well as the Decapolis (with which we shall deal later). Judea, of course, was under the direct rule of the procurators. Jerusalem is mentioned in an attempt to indicate that the religious capital, where the temple was located, was not apart from the movement. The Idumeans had many bad memories attached to their name (cf. Ps. 137:7-9), and the reign of Herod the Great (an Idumean) had not brought about the complete disappearance of the ancestral hatred. Yet even the Idumeans had heard of the things that were happening on the shores of the Sea of Galilee.

All of the regions named so far had been, and were still, imbued with Judaism, regardless of the infiltration of Hellenism, which by then had become solidly implanted everywhere. But here new territories appear: Tyre and Sidon, the two great Mediterranean ports, whose religious and political foundations differed from those of the other regions mentioned. Rome had been installed there since 63 B.C. In the temples the Canaanite gods were still worshiped (although they bore new names and were worshiped in the Western mode). Tyre and Sidon were so near and in such close contact with Upper Galilee that it is not surprising to find some people coming from those regions.

❷ A tradition locates "the Mount" at Karn Hattin, some four and a half miles west of the Sea of Galilee. But the tradition is indefensible and should be dismissed without further ado. This basaltic hill whose western slope faces on the Wadi el-Haram entered into history for quite another reason: it was the battlefield where, on July 14, 1187, Saladin crushed the army of Franks commanded by Guy de Lusignan.

The authors of the Synoptic Gospels considered that they could not take time to give the location of the Mount, and that

41. Tyre.   42. Karn Hattin.

1 *You are the salt of the earth (Matthew 5:13)*
2 *A city set on a hill cannot be hid (Matthew 5:14)*

to do so was useless anyway, since everybody knew where it was. It was *the* mountain (Matt. 5:1; Mark 3:13; Luke 6:12).

Moreover, they did not all situate the same event there. For Matthew, it was essentially the site of the teaching and of the giving of the Lord's Prayer. Mark locates there the choosing of the twelve, which is confirmed by Luke. On the other hand, Luke situates the teaching not on "the Mount" but on "a level place" (Luke 6:17), which must have been close by. Thus, only one thing may be said about this important event in the Galilean ministry: it took place in an out-of-the-way spot, probably to the northwest of the lake, that is, in the back-country of Capernaum.

❶ The more I live in the Orient, the less I understand this saying. To be sure, it has been illustrated for me many times, when, after a rainfall, the ground dries and is covered with great white sheets. But truly, this saying escapes me. Salt, whose properties the homily extols, is less than desired by the people of the Orient. It is salt that renders the soil completely sterile and unproductive, it is salt that renders water undrinkable. We experienced this both at Mari and

at Telloh, where the salty soil permits nothing to grow and where the water, which fills up the trenches of our excavations, is completely useless.

The "salt of the earth". . . yes. But only on condition that it is taken up and utilized far from the soil that it renders unfruitful.

❷ Jesus was perhaps thinking of Safaad (ancient Sepheth), which is situated on the summit of a hill (2750 ft.) set off by two ravines, and which looks out over an extensive panorama. At the same time, it could be recognized from afar. Jesus had only to raise his arm and point to the city: his listeners would have seen it easily.

43. The "salt of the earth."

1 *Nor do men light a lamp and put it under a bushel, but on a stand (Matthew 5:15)*

2 *Till heaven and earth pass away, not an iota, not a dot, will pass from the law until all is accomplished (Matthew 5:18)*

44. Palestinian lamp.

❶ The Canaanite, Israelite, and, later, Jewish lamps were generally of terra-cotta. Their shape varied over the centuries (which enables one to date them), but their height remained constant: a few centimeters. The lamp was a small bowl with a flat bottom and two openings: one in the center, into which the oil was poured; the other at one end, through which the wick was inserted. A symmetrical handle enabled one to grasp it easily. The duration of illumination was limited by the small reservoir, and the brightness of the light was also rather restrained. Thus, in order to have more light, one had to put the lamp on a stand. It is curious that so far no excavator has been able to identify this accessory except when it is of metal, in which case it corresponds to a metal lamp (usually of bronze). But metal lamps were used only in worship services or by patrician families. The common people used only the clay lamp. At first it was without ornamentation, but in later times it was decorated with geometric, floral, and vegetable combinations and even with bawdy motifs.

❷ The accomplishment that is at issue here, and that the examples are intended to clarify, is the unfolding, to their ultimate consequences, of the guiding principles of the Law (*Bible du Centenaire*). In the square characters of Hebrew, adopted at the beginning of the Persian period (5th century B.C.), the *yod* (Greek *iota*) was the smallest letter of the alphabet. It was in the form of a tiny hook, and was placed in line with the top of the letters. The "dot" ["stroke," NEB] was probably the miniscule extension which enabled one to distinguish, for example, the *he* [ה] from the *heth* [ח]. These two extremely trifling things were used to characterize better the severity of an attitude.

1 *The judge, the guard, the prison (Matthew 5:25–26)*
2 *You shall not commit adultery (Matthew 5:27)*
3 *But I say to you, Do not resist (Matthew 5:39)*

❶ This procedure is still in effect today. The seraglios [sultans' palaces] are always full of individuals who come before the judge to air their domestic quarrels, their property disputes, their tribal hatreds. And justice is speedy; the individual appears before the judge on the same day that he has been summoned, and it is possible that he will be led off to prison by the guard ["constable," NEB]. The prison often adjoins the court, at least in smaller cities. It should be added that, in the Orient, a stay of several weeks behind bars is not considered at all degrading. This is all part of the hazards of life and no one can predict that it will not happen to him one day. The fine had to be paid down to the last *quadrans* (the fourth part of an *as*), which was a small bronze coin worth about a quarter of a cent.

❷ This was one of the ten commandments of the Law (Exod. 20:14; Deut. 5: 18). Ancient legislation was very severe on this score. Assyrian laws prescribed the death penalty for the woman and her accomplice. Among the Hittites, the husband had the right to choose the punishment, either death or severe mutilation, but also to pardon. At Mari, when there was some doubt concerning guilt, the wife was thrown into the "God-River." If she emerged, it was because she was innocent. If not, the drowning was the punishment.

❸ The Mosaic law was explicit: "You shall give life for life, eye for eye, tooth for tooth, hand for hand, foot for foot, burn for burn, wound for wound, stripe for stripe" (Exod. 21:23–25). Israel made no innovation here. Babylonian law was equally clear. The Code of Hammurabi prescribes: "If a seignor has destroyed the eye of a member of the aristocracy, they shall destroy his eye" (196); "If he has broken another seignor's bone, they shall break his bone" (197); "If a seignor has knocked out a tooth of a seignor of his own rank, they shall knock out his tooth" (200).[1]

Such prescriptions could be cited at length. Every case is provided for, and this equivalence is respected each time. Jesus opposed to this vengeful legalism a very different attitude: to accept for oneself the worst of injustices. Even more: to return good for evil. To do this is to attain perfection. Probably only saints can be successful in this.

[1] [Translation by Theophile J. Meek, in *The Ancient Near East: An Anthology of Texts and Pictures*, ed. James B. Pritchard ("Princeton Paperback," Princeton University Press, 1965). Meek translates the word *awelum* as "seignor," meaning "any free man of standing."

1 *Do not lay up for yourselves treasures on earth, where moth and rust consume and where thieves break in and steal (Matthew 6:19)*

2 *Do not be anxious about your life, what you shall eat or what you shall drink, nor about your body, what you shall put on (Matthew 6:25)*

3 *A cubit (Matthew 6:27)*

❶ In a sense, we can understand the damage done by moths, but the reference to rust is vaguer. However, this is easily explained if we remember that tools and many utensils were of iron, a metal which is quite sensitive to humidity. It was very difficult to fight against it, and many objects attacked by it ultimately crumbled into dust. As for the thieves breaking in, this was a common occurrence. It was frequent because the constructions often were of dried mud, and the walls offered only a slight resistance. At Telloh, in 1930, a thief broke through the wall of one of our rooms and thus gained entrance to the house without having to break open the door.

45. Bedouin costume.

❷ It should be recognized that the Palestinian of Jesus' day, like the Bedouin of today, lived a simple, rustic life and had limited needs. The Bedouin's clothing is composed of three pieces: a tunic undergarment, a mantle, and a *keffieh* for the head. These garments last for many years, since wear and tear is minor. As for the customary food, this is not a problem: some domestic herbs, an onion, a leek, some radishes, a few dates and figs. As drink, water from the wadi or from the lake, or milk from camels, sheep, or goats. A few coins, a few piastres, suffice.

❸ Obviously this was not the metrical system, but a very ingenious means and method of measuring. From the smallest to the largest: the finger, the palm, the span (from the end of the thumb to the end of

41

1 *The lilies of the field (Matthew 6:28)*

2 *The grass of the field, which today is alive and tomorrow is thrown into the oven (Matthew 6:30)*

46. Woman carrying ratab.

the little finger). The cubit was a royal measurement and was used in architecture. The sides of the large and fine square baked bricks of the royal constructions of Mesopotamia were one cubit in length. The dimensions of the temple of Jerusalem were given in cubits. Jesus, in order to show that worries were of no help, gave this example: no man, by being anxious, can add a cubit to his height ("a foot to his height," NEB) or better, according to some versions, "to the span of life" (RSV).

❶ In April, all Palestine is a tapestry of flowers: large yellow marguerites, red or mauve anemones, white or pink cyclamens. In all this floral abundance, what were the "lilies of the field"? Anemones or cyclamens, we believe. A flower of a few days, it blooms in the morning sun, is "withered" by the wind of midday, and begins to fade at the first harsh rays of the implacable afternoon sun (cf. Ps. 90:6).

❷ In the Orient, everything is burned; the vegetation is rare, and therefore all the more precious. Yet, precious or not, the fire must be lit in order to heat the "oven" on which the bread is baked. This is probably what Jesus was referring to. In the court of each house there is even today a small earthen installation (*tannour*), with a dome open at the top. One starts by heating its interior walls with a fire of *ratab* (grass of the fields). When this fuel is consumed, the women quickly stick the thin, circular cakes of daily bread against the burning-hot areas. This operation is continued as long as the oven is hot or until there is a sufficient amount of bread. Each family makes its own bread in this fashion. The task is reserved to the women, who must also be sure that enough *ratab* has been gathered and brought home.

42

1 *The speck and the log (Matthew 7:3–5)*
2 *Do not give dogs what is holy; and do not throw your pearls before swine (Matthew 7:6)*
3 *Loaf and stone, fish and serpent (Matthew 7:9–10)*
4 *Enter by the narrow gate (Matthew 7:13)*

❶ These are two concrete items, widely used, yet they are of such different sizes that nothing could have been better chosen to illustrate the lesson Jesus had in mind. Jesus often employed this teaching method: the speck and the log, the gnat and the camel (Matt. 23:24), the needle and the camel (Matt. 19:24). Once again, the two terms of comparison are taken from daily life. Wheat straw[1] is used as fodder for the cattle, in the making of bricks (cf. Exod. 5:7), and in the preparation of *motal* (the Bedouin "yellow coal," cakes of animal dung mixed with chopped straw and dried in the sun). Logs supported the terrace roof. The small straw and the large log are both part of the structure of the house.

❷ Dogs and swine were unclean animals. Even today, Muslim and Jew do not eat pork. As for dogs, if one used them to guard the house or the tent, one had to be careful not to pet or even to touch them. Jesus used this example in order to make clear that one had no right to profane holy things.

❸ Bread and fish were the two primary elements of food for those who lived on the shores of the lake (Matt. 14:17). Stone and

[1] The French version has *"paille"* (straw) where the English reads "speck."

47. Woman bundling straw.

serpent, two plagues of the Orient, were frequently found together. All that is missing is the scorpion, which is found in Luke (11:12).

❹ There are two passageways at Pompeii which beautifully illustrate this text: side by side are a large gate, which is used by almost all of the tourists, and a small gate that is ordinarily ignored. At Bethlehem, the entrance to the Church of the Nativity is low rather than narrow. The doors to the houses of the indigenous population are always low and narrow. This is undoubtedly to reduce to an absolute minimum the space through which sun or cold can enter.

43

1 *Sheep and wolf; grapes and thorns; figs and thistles (Matthew 7:15–16)*

2 *Every tree that does not bear good fruit is cut down and thrown into the fire (Matthew 7:19)*

3 *The house built on the rock (Matthew 7:24–27; Luke 6:47–49)*

4 *And Jesus went about all the cities and villages, teaching in their synagogues and preaching the gospel of the kingdom, and healing (Matthew 9:35; Mark 6:6)*

❶ In a few words we have both the good and bad fauna and produce of Palestine: the flocks of sheep and the wolves that prowl everywhere; the grapes of Hebron and the thorns of Gerizim; the figs of Bethany and the thistles that run down toward the blue waters of the Sea of Galilee.

❷ Before the advent of "petroleum civilization," the lack of combustible material led to these harsh measures. In the West, we hesitate to do this. We never cut down a fruit tree unless it is dead. In Palestine it was different. It was not a matter of a useless fire, such as a farmer ignites to burn off brush and stumps; rather, it was a fire burning on the stones of the hearth, about which the family warmed itself. Olive, walnut, and apricot were the three types of trees most used in Syria for firewood before the advent of fuel oil. Unless I am mistaken, the walnut outclassed the other two, both in price and in heat output.

❸ The houses of the village of Siloam are built solidly on rock. They have no fear of the rain that falls in torrents from January to March. Nor, probably, did they fear the Kidron when it flowed, for they were located above its bed. Wind, rain, flood: such is the normal order in Palestine. The west wind brings the rains and the rains almost instantaneously swell the wadis; the wadis, dry just moments before, are filled with surging walls of reddish water which brutally sweeps everything along with it. We have witnessed two automobiles, engaged in an ill-advised attempt to cross a wadi, swept away like straws. The Bedouins know — they are very careful not to pitch their tents on the sand (admittedly comfortable) of a dry brook.

❹ This passage indicates that Galilee had a high density of population. The Jewish historian Josephus confirms this, reckoning the number of urban centers at 240. The more important cities must have had their own synagogues (*Beth ha-keneset*, "the house of the assembly") where, since the Exile (6th century B.C.), the people have gathered on the sabbath. One of the best-preserved synagogues in Galilee is that of Kefr Birim, from which the Louvre has a lintel with inscription. The Gospels report numerous healings by Jesus of lepers, paralytics, and demoniacs.

1 *They came . . . to the country of the Gerasenes. And . . . there met him out of the tombs a man with an unclean spirit (Mark 5:1–2)*

48. Tomb in the rock.

❶ Although this region undoubtedly was on the east shore of the Sea of Galilee, its exact location remains in doubt. The manuscripts give several readings: Gadarenes, Gerasenes, Gergesenes, which implies the three different cities of Gadara, Gerasa, Gergesa.

Gadara is one of the cities of the Decapolis, identified with Umm Qeis, located to the east of the Jordan and rather far inland from the Sea. Gerasa is also of the Decapolis; it is undoubtedly the present city of Jerash, southeast of the Sea and much too far away to be considered as a possible site. Gergesa, finally, was quite near the Sea, at a place today called Kersa. The demoniac (two of them, according to Matt. 8:28) lived in one of the many tombs cut into the rock. This was a very spacious shelter, since these tombs were generally family sepulchers.

45

1 *And as he sat at table in the house, behold, many tax collectors and sinners came and sat down with Jesus and his disciples (Matthew 9:10)*

2 *The flute players, and the crowd making a tumult (Matthew 9:23)*

One could find no better place for a mentally deranged person, one finally abandoned by his fellow countrymen who were only too happy to be rid of him. There were asylums and even prisons where these unfortunates lived enchained in cells. An example, although from a much later date, was the Mauristan Argoun at Aleppo. One cannot visit this prison, which was built in the 14th century, without experiencing as much fear as pity. The madmen of Gergesa were at least at liberty and, when they wanted to, could breathe free air.

The next scene is well known: the unclean spirits, at Jesus' command, came out of the demoniac and entered the swine. The swine, in turn, ran over the cliff that overlooks the Sea and were drowned. A herd of swine (numbering about two thousand head according to Mark 5:13) in this country was not surprising. For the hellenized people of the Decapolis, swine were not unclean animals as they were for the Jews (Lev. 11:7). Quite the contrary, swine must have provided an important source of income, since their flesh was eaten by the Roman soldiers of the occupation forces.

❶ If one is not acquainted with oriental customs, the ease of manners implied in this account must seem enormous. Even today, when a guest of note arrives in a village and is received in the house of a notable (a civil or religious chief), all the peasants hasten to the place without having been invited. Squatting in a tight ring around the walls of the reception hall, they silently observe the proceedings. They are simply spectators and supernumeraries, for the coffee or tea of hospitality is seldom served to them, but it is considered good form to have them present.

❷ The scene is set this time in the house of one of the rulers of the synagogue, Jairus (Mark 5:22; Luke 8:41), whose daughter has just died. It was the custom that immediately after a death demonstrations of sorrow unfolded. There were not only professional mourners recruited for the occasion, but also neighbors, who demonstrated noisily. Matthew also refers to flute players. The presence of musicians at this time may seem incongruous. Yet the custom is provided for and codified in the Mishnah. Moreover, a relief on a Roman tomb represents mourning women grouped about a corpse lying on a couch, and a seated man playing the flute at the foot of the catafalque.[1]

[1] Reproduced in *Views of the Biblical World*, 5, *The New Testament*, p. 40.

1 *And as Jesus passed on from there, two blind men followed him, crying aloud, "Have mercy on us, Son of David" (Matthew 9:27)*

2 *Healing of the woman suffering from a hemorrhage (Matthew 9:20–22; Mark 5:25–34; Luke 8:43–48)*

3 *The harvest is plentiful (Matthew 9:37–38)*

❶ This is an everyday scene in Palestine or in Syria. In these countries, where not so long ago trachoma wreaked havoc, blind men wail and implore pity from the passersby all day long. We remember one man, on his knees at the foot of the narrow street leading up to the Holy Sepulcher, who waited with upraised hands from dawn to dusk. His litany of supplications gushed forth, always the same, with a quavering voice that accented even more the two empty sockets.

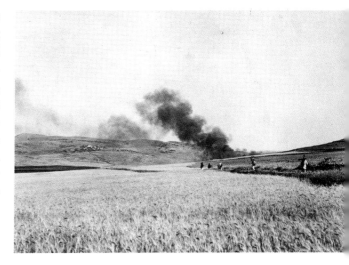

49. Harvest ablaze in Samaria.

❷ As Jesus was making his way to the home of Jairus, the ruler of the synagogue, a sick woman came out of the crowd and touched the fringe of his mantle. She was instantly healed. The Mari tablets have revealed this same belief in the importance of the fringes of the mantle: in order to conclude an agreement, the fringes of the mantle were knotted

Among the Assyrians, the mantle was the substitute for the king. Even in the modern West at certain funerals, the uniform or the professorial robe of the deceased is laid upon the coffin.

❸ The harvest took place at the end of spring during the month of May. The hills of Samaria were all "white" (John 4:35) — of a golden white — with grains of wheat and rye awaiting the harvesters. Compared to the vastness of the fields covered with grain, the harvesters were not very numerous, especially considering the tools, which only now have begun to be less primitive. Then the men had nothing but sickles, and the women worked behind them, in a line, bending over to gather the grain.

1 *No one who puts his hand to the plow and looks back is fit for the kingdom of God (Luke 9:62)*

2 *Take no gold, nor silver, nor copper in your belts, no bag for your journey, nor two tunics, nor sandals, nor a staff (Matthew 10:9–10; Luke 9:3)*

❶ Up until recent times, the plow had not varied for some three thousand years. Essentially, it was composed of two pieces of wood: a beam attached to the yoke and a coulter which was seated in an iron share. This tool scratched the soil more than it turned it, but that was sufficient. The sower could then sow his grain.

❷ Jesus is saying that the disciples should take nothing of what the traveler usually carried with him. Money was carried in a special pouch in the belt: the coins could have been of gold (the *aureus*), of silver (the *denarius* or the *shekel*), or of copper (the *as* and its various denominations). The bag was a knitted woolen pouch which was hung over the shoulder and in which one carried bread. The Bedouin, when he is traveling, rarely has more than his mantle with his tunic underneath; his mantle serves as a cover at night (cf. Exod. 22:27). As for the sandals, most of the time the nomad does not keep them on; thus he is able to move faster and also does not wear out the sandals. Matthew and Luke both proscribe the staff, but Mark (6:8) includes it. This is an accessory of travel. It is not a rigid and thick branch, but a supple and flexible cane. When slipped behind the back under

50. Plowman in Samaria.

1 *As you enter the house, salute it (Matthew 10:12)*
2 *And whoever gives . . . even a cup of cold water (Matthew 10:42)*

the arms, it works as a brace and makes one's gait more rapid and supple. Jesus' instructions, therefore, were the opposite of all the customs. This was not the first time. There is a twofold explanation of this passage: the laborer is worth his hire; and the missionary must be free of all encumbrances.

❶ Hospitality is a golden rule in the Orient, and, at least in the villages, travelers are accommodated without charge. There is often a room reserved for this purpose which is the "guest house." They tell you: "My house is yours. What is mine is yours." This is true, but one should not abuse the generosity. In Iraq, you say, *"Salam aleikoum"* ("May health be yours"). Your host responds with the same formula, but reversed: *"Aleikoum salam."* The greeting continues with "How are you?" (*"Kef halak"* or *"Schlon kefak"*). This must be repeated several times as one addresses each person present (beginning with the highest in rank and dignity). Once these civilities are disposed of, all that remains is to enjoy the welcome, which is always generous, even among the most wretched and least fortunate. All that the Bedouin has — water, *leben* (a type of yogurt) — he will bring to you, even though later he may have to do without.

❷ This statement is not understood fully except in the Orient, where water is very rare and becomes even more precious because the need to quench the thirst is great, indeed sometimes overbearing. The traveler or anyone who asks for water is never refused, even when the cistern which has caught the rainfall of the season is almost empty, or when there is little water in the spring or well where the women go each evening to draw water (cf. Gen. 24:11). This water is given to one in a metal cup (Gr. *poterion*) or better, in a jug with a lip on it (a sort of water pitcher) which enables one to pour the water straight down the throat.

51. Plowman and sower in Samaria.

1 *Shake off the dust from your feet (Matthew 10:14; Mark 6:11; Luke 9:5)*

2 *Behold, those who wear soft raiment are in kings' houses (Matthew 11:8; Luke 7:25)*

3 *Proclaim upon the housetops (Matthew 10:27)*

❶ A refusal of hospitality seemed unthinkable. But the Evangelists are unanimous in recalling Jesus' instructions in case hospitality was refused the disciples. This gesture was as realistic as symbolic, for dust is ever present. It is especially abundant at the end of the dry season, in October, before the first rains. There is then a thick layer of dust which has accumulated since April. In order not to bring dust into his tent, the Bedouin always takes off his sandals before entering and walking on his mats or his *kelim* (goatskin rugs). Despite this care, it is quite difficult to avoid dust in the tent. In leaving, those who had not been well received would therefore shake the dust from their feet, in order not to carry it with them but rather to leave it with its owners (cf. Luke 10:11). Thus no one could claim to have given anything to them! Paul and Barnabas made the same gesture of scorn vis-à-vis the Jews of Antioch of Pisidia (Acts 13:51).

❷ Although Jesus alludes to the "kings" of Palestine, there were only two such kings: Herod Antipas, who resided at Tiberias and Machaerus; and Philip, whose palace must have been at Caesarea Philippi. The remainder of the region was under the jurisdiction of the procurator Pilate, who lived at Caesarea by the Sea.

❸ During the summer in Palestine, one lives almost as much on the roof as in the street, especially after nightfall. The interior of the houses is so hot that one spends the night on a bed or mattress on the terrace-roof (of hard, rolled earth). No attention is paid to the world of the neighbor, who is doing precisely the same thing. A fence of reeds or palm branches provides a bit of privacy. All of the houses touch, and the roofs also adjoin. News passes easily from one to the other, both at the time when the city prepares for sleep and at the time when it awakes in the morning.

52. Children piping and dancing.

1 *This generation . . . is like children sitting in the market places and calling to their playmates, "We piped to you, and you did not dance" (Matthew 11:16–17)*

2 *When the unclean spirit . . . comes he finds [the house] empty, swept, and put in order. Then he goes and brings with him seven other spirits (Matthew 12:43–45; Luke 11:24–26)*

3 *My yoke is easy, and my burden is light (Matthew 11:30)*

❶ This is a common sight everywhere, and one which we have often witnessed. A child, seated on the ground, will bring out a small flute (two ends of reeds joined together) and tirelessly begin to repeat a four-note theme. His playmates will then get up and begin to improvise a dance, clapping their hands to give a lively rhythm to the dance. This manifestation of joy is frequent. On the other hand, we have never witnessed the contrary scene ["we wailed, and you did not mourn"], but there is no reason to doubt that it also was common.

❷ The background of this passage is that demonical world with which Jesus was frequently at grips. It is quite probable that allusion is made here to a belief which was ultimately rooted in Mesopotamian magic; according to this belief, "the Seven" were the most redoubtable of the evil powers. Each of the Seven had a name (in Sumerian as in Akkadian), and the generic appellation (*utukku*) was ordinarily followed by the epithet "evil" (*limnu*). A very complicated ritual was prescribed in order to exorcise the sick person and to rid him of these undesirable spirits. A famous plaque, from the collection of Clercq, illustrates the various stages of treatment. Jesus' words can be understood only in this oriental setting.

❸ These two images are from the life of Jesus' day: pulling was done by animals (the yoke) and all loads (the burden) were transported on the backs of asses, mules, camels, and also on the backs of men. (This is true even today.) In 1965, at both Jerusalem and Beirut, we saw laborers with enormous loads on their backs, fastened across their fronts by large straps. This

53.   Plaque from the collection of Clercq.

1 *It is only by Beelzebul, the prince of demons, that this man casts out demons (Matthew 12:24; Mark 3:22)*

2 *A sower went out to sow (Matthew 13:3–8; Mark 4:3–9; Luke 8:5–8)*

3 *The seed scattered upon the ground (Mark 4:26–29)*

4 *The enemy came and sowed weeds (Matthew 13:24–30)*

same procedure was current among the Sumerians, as is illustrated by the "Standard" of Ur (mid-3rd millennium B.C.).[1]

❶ The Gospels have retained the true name of this deity that some have wanted, wrongly, to identify with Baal-zebub ("Lord of the Flies"), the god of Ekron (II Kings 1:2). This Baal-zebub undoubtedly never existed and there is every reason to assume that the Philistine city already worshiped a Baal-zebul, who was none other than the Aliyan-Baal of Ras Shamra, the god of springs; his habitation (*zebul*) was located in the depths of the earth (Dussaud).

❷ Three quarters of the seed was lost: on the path, where the birds ate it; among the rocks, where there was not enough soil to give adequate depth to the roots; in the thorns, that is to say, all the varieties of thorny weeds that choke off the useful plants. Happily, the last quarter fell on good soil and produced a fine crop. The numbers indicated (hundredfold, sixtyfold, thirtyfold), correspond precisely to what is

[1] [See Jack Finegan, *Light from the Ancient Past* (2nd ed.; Princeton University Press, 1959), for a reproduction (Fig. 16) and a description (p. 42) of the Standard.]

known of the soil of Palestine. In Judea, seed does indeed produce thirtyfold, and sixty to a hundredfold has been known on certain plains (Esdraelon, Gennesaret). As to the explication which Jesus gives (Matt. 13:18–23; Mark 4:13–20; Luke 8:11–15), it is admirably drawn from the facts.

❸ As soon as the man has sown the seed on the ground, it is out of his control. At the end of a given time, without his having had anything to do with it, the harvest is ready to be gathered in. This is a magnificent illustration of the work of creation. But what is its true meaning? The exegetes have asked themselves this question, but it undoubtedly did not seem so complicated to the Galileans who heard it.

❹ This parable is the clearest explanation of evil and the most lucid response to the "problem of evil" that has perplexed all men: "An enemy has done this." The mustard seed, the smallest of all seeds (Matt. 13:31–32; Mark 4:30–32), ultimately grows into a tree. The leaven (Matt. 13:33; Luke 13:21) causes dough to rise. These two examples, one from nature and the other from domestic life, show the greatness of the result in relation to the starting point and to the powerful, though hidden, action of a ferment.

1 *The treasure hidden in a field (Matthew 13:44)*
2 *The pearl of great value (Matthew 13:45–46)*
3 *A net thrown into the sea (Matthew 13:47)*
4 *The daughter of Herodias danced (Matthew 14:6; Mark 6:22)*

54. Net drawn up on the beach.

by some unknown person some two thousand years ago. At Mari, in 1965, we discovered a jar full of a Sumerian "treasure"! Jesus, in choosing this example, could well have been alluding to a precise fact, known to his hearers.

❷ Pearls were not of Palestinian origin; they came from the shores of the Red Sea and from the Arabian coast.

❶ During every age, at times of crisis, men hide their most valuable possessions in the earth, with the obvious intention of retrieving them when the danger is past. But it sometimes happens that the owner dies in the meantime, or that he forgets the exact spot where he hid his goods and thus finds it impossible to retrieve them. Many archaeologists, to their joy, have made discoveries which can be explained only in this way. In the basement of a house at Larsa, in 1933, we discovered a jar full of pure silver ingots. At Qumran, in 1955, Father Roland de Vaux had an identical experience: he found three containers filled with a "treasure" of 561 silver coins buried under the earthen floor of a room. At Mount Carmel, in 1960, there was the discovery of nearly 5000 coins (shekels and half-shekels), left

❸ The net is let down between two boats; when it is full, it is drawn up on the shore by a column of half-naked men. Then the catch is sorted and the worthless fish are tossed back into the sea. Between the wars, we often witnessed this operation along the Mediterranean between Haifa and Acre.

❹ Herodias was the granddaughter of Herod the Great. According to Josephus, she had first been the wife of a Herod who was the son of Herod the Great and thus at the same time her uncle![1] From this marriage she had a daughter, Salome. According to the Evangelists Matthew (14:3) and Mark (6:17), Herodias had become the wife of Philip, whom she later left in order

[1] See *infra*, Table I, "Herodian Dynasty." [In Josephus, cf. *Antiquities*, 18.5.1.]

53

1 *The multiplication of the loaves (Matthew 14:15–21; Mark 6:35–44; Luke 9:12–17; John 6:5–13)*

2 *The fourth watch of the night (Matthew 14:25)*

to live with Herod Antipas.[1] Philip must then later have married Salome. It was Salome who appeared before the guests of Herod Antipas and who obtained from the kinglet, as a reward for her performance, the head of the Baptist. The Romans were very strict regarding this type of spectacle, and permitted it only to professionals. It is curious to note that even today, in the Orient, only women whom one considers of ill repute perform in public. But at the banquet of Herod, it was a princess of royal blood who demonstrated her agility.

❶ This scene should probably be located on the left bank of the Jordan, in an out-of-the-way region not too far from Bethsaida. Loaves (or, rather, thin cakes) of bread and fish, as we have already said, constituted the customary food of the people of the region. The "grass" which is mentioned indicates that the scene took place in spring, between March and May; at other times there would be scarcely anything but rocks in that "lonely place." The crowd that had gathered was so large and it was so late in the day that the disciples wondered if it would not be better to disperse

[1] We accept from the two Evangelists this information which some exegetes consider to be erroneous. Cf. *supra*, comment on Luke 3:19–20.

the people. Thus they could go into neighboring towns and buy provisions, which no one seemed to have brought along. It was then that the miracle took place. The account contains a very expressive detail: the number of guests is reckoned by all four Evangelists to have been five thousand people. But it is made quite clear that this number includes only the "men." Women and children were not counted, which conforms perfectly with the oriental mentality.

❷ Among the nomadic and pastoral peoples, the night is just as important as the day. On one hand, it is a source of dangers, and one understands the interrogation in Isaiah (21:11), "Watchman, what of the night?" On the other hand, it is the time chosen for traveling, with the moon lighting the trails and guiding the caravans. The lunar god (Nannar among the Sumerians, Sin among the Semites) was one of the greatest of the Mesopotamian gods. Between sundown and sunrise, the Romans had four watches, one every three hours. Thus when Jesus rejoins his disciples, walking on the water, it is 3 A.M. and dawn is about to break. The boat probably left from the vicinity of Bethsaida and was headed for the west shore in order to land at Gennesaret (vs. 34).

1 *Washing the hands before the meal (Matthew 15:2; Mark 7:5)*

2 *"He who speaks evil of father or mother, let him surely die" (Matthew 15:4)*

3 *The blind leading the blind (Matthew 15:14)*

4 *The district of Tyre and Sidon (Matthew 15:21–28; Mark 7:24–30)*

❶ These ablutions had become rituals and were observed by the Pharisees. Undoubtedly, they had arisen from practical necessity. Since the ancients used neither forks nor spoons to eat their meals, they were quite naturally inclined to wash their hands before approaching the heaping platters. Mark says further that the hands were washed "up to the elbow" (7:3). Some exegetes contest this translation,[1] but the detail can be explained easily by a practice still in force. Today the Arabs of the desert, who serve themselves only with the right hand, roll the sleeve of their tunic up to the elbow, in order not to get their sleeve soiled when they "dip their hand in the dish" (cf. Mark 14:20; Matt. 26:23).

❷ This prescription from Exodus (21:17), repeated by Jesus, was inspired by much more ancient laws. In the 18th century B.C. Hammurabi, the king of Babylon, prescribed capital punishment for anyone who shirked filial love.

❸ No matter how paradoxical this may seem, we are convinced that Jesus was citing here a current example. At Jerusalem, we have often encountered two blind men leading each other. Figure 55 shows two *ulemas*, identified by the white band around their heads. *Ulemas* rarely "fall into a pit," for collective compassion helps them to avoid the false steps, the curbs of the sidewalks, the conduits into which they would almost inevitably fall, even though otherwise they could succeed in leading each other almost perfectly, from alley to alley, from house to house, their eyes extinguished forever.

❹ During the time of Jesus, the two ancient Phoenician ports on the Mediterranean were still the center of a great commercial

[1] [Neither RSV nor NEB includes the phrase.]

55. "The blind leading the blind."

activity. Tyre had ceased to be an island from the time of Alexander the Great (4th century B.C.), since, in order to conquer it, the Macedonian general had attached it to the mainland by means of an immense dike. Even though the prosperity of the city was no longer as great as it had been in the time of Ezekiel (Ezek. 27), it was far from having "come to a dreadful end" (Ezek. 27:36). Sidon, crowned by gardens of orange and apricot groves, was permanently in greenery and flowers. With their pagan deities (Melchart at Tyre, Eshmun at Sidon), the two metropolises hardly seemed prepared or disposed to receive the gospel message, despite the Jewish colonies in their midst. Yet it was there that Jesus both rendered justice to a woman ("Canaanite," according to Matt. 15:22; "Syrophoenician," according to Mark 7:26) and healed her daughter. When he left the region, he had occasion to compare it favorably with certain cities in Galilee which were hostile to his activity (Matt. 11:21–22; Luke 10:13–14) and which would be dealt with more harshly on "the day of judgment" than the two pagan cities.

56.   Syrophoenician women from the sarcophagus of the mourners (Sidon). *Museum of Istanbul.*

1 *Then he returned from the region of Tyre, and went through Sidon to the Sea of Galilee, through the region of the Decapolis (Mark 7:31)*

57. Lake Huleh.

● The itinerary is surprising, for Sidon is some 25 miles north of Tyre, and if the return took place by way of the Decapolis, as the Evangelist indicates, it would require a major detour. In any case, this is not the direct route back to Galilee (and especially to the region of the lake). Yet we must take the text as it stands and allow Jesus the right to go where he wanted and where he intended to go. From the Mediterranean coast, he would have had to go to the valley of the Upper Jordan by first crossing the heights of southern Lebanon. This would have been done by taking one of the existing passes (which we took in 1928, since the network of roads had not yet then been improved and extended). From the valley of the Upper Jordan to the northern shore of Lake Huleh and south of Mount Hermon one passes without difficulty into the region of the Decapolis (the area already discussed in relation to the Gergesenes). As its name indicates, the Decapolis was a confederation of ten cities.

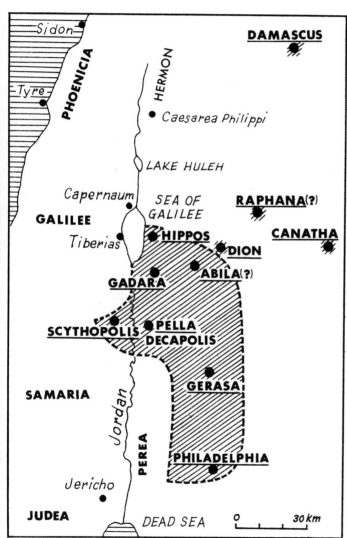

These cities had received the imprint of Hellenistic civilization, and the Romans, on the initiative of Pompey (63 B.C.), had accorded the region a special status (undoubtedly to help root out the Jewish influence).

These ten cities were, from north to south, to the east of the Jordan: Damascus, Canatha (today el-Qanawat, at Jebel Druze), Dion (Tell el-Ashari), Hippos (Qalat el-Husn), Gadara (Umm Qeis), Pella (Khirbet Fahil), Gerasa (Jerash), Philadelphia (Amman, capital of Jordan); to the west of the Jordan, and southwest of the Sea of Galilee: Scythopolis (ancient Beth-Shan, today Beisan, at Tell el-Husn). There is some doubt regarding the missing tenth city. It was perhaps Raphana (in Batanea) or Abila, between Gadara and Dion. This city is not to be confused with the Abila of Lysanias, which was northwest of Damascus. Although eight of these cities were grouped fairly close together, two were rather remote: Damascus and Canatha.

In returning from Tyre and Sidon, moreover, Jesus could not have entered the region of the Decapolis except by passing through the territory belonging to the tetrarch Philip, brother of Herod Antipas (see map, Fig. 5).

58.   Map of the Decapolis.

1 *And Jesus went on with his disciples, to the villages of Caesarea Philippi (Mark 8:27)*

2 *The Transfiguration. On a high mountain (Matthew 17:1–8; Mark 9:2–8; Luke 9:28–36)*

 The capital of the tetrarchy of Philip was Caesarea, a city built in 3 B.C. by Philip and named in honor of the Roman emperor. The whole country was dedicated to the worship of the god Pan, whence came the name of a small town nearby, Paneas. This name survives in Banias, the modern name of Caesarea. In a cliff near one of the sources of the Jordan, one sees even today five niches cut into the rock, designed to contain statues. In front of the cave dedicated to Pan, overlooking the source, Herod the Great built a temple in honor of Augustus. Caesarea Philippi (called thus to distinguish it from Caesarea by the Sea) was, according to Matthew (16:13–18), the place where Peter made his "confession," to which Jesus replied, "You are Peter, and on this rock I will build my church." It should be recognized that the background served admirably for this.

 The location of the Transfiguration is not specified. However, according to Mark, Jesus and the disciples had previously been in the region of Caesarea Philippi, and since it is not said that they had left this region, scholars have sought to locate there the site of the Transfiguration. There is a "high mountain" nearby, Mount Hermon (9166 ft.). Tradition, on the contrary, has from the 3rd century located the site on Mount Tabor, where a Byzantine church was constructed. Tabor is isolated, but it cannot

59. Mt. Tabor.

1 *The signs of the times (Matthew 16:2–3)*

2 *When you see a cloud rising in the west, you say at once, "A shower is coming" (Luke 12:54)*

3 *And when you see the south wind blowing, you say, "There will be a scorching heat" (Luke 12:55)*

4 *Often he falls into the fire, and often into the water (Matthew 17:15)*

easily be called a "high mountain," for it rises only less than 1000 feet above the plain. Then again, one could not really say that it was "apart" (Mark 9:2), since we know from Josephus that there was a fortress on the summit during Jesus' day. Consequently, in our opinion, Mount Hermon is better suited to the needs of the account, and one of its foothills was probably the place to which Jesus led his disciples. In this confrontation between the bearer of the New Covenant and two heroes of the Old Covenant, Mount Hermon had become a new Sinai.

60.   A child fallen into the fire.

❶ The ancients were past masters in the art of "interpreting the appearance of the sky," since all of their activity depended on good or bad weather. This was especially true during winter, when the climate was so unstable. As with us, a red sky in the evening was a good omen for the next day, whereas a red sky in the morning did not bode well for the remainder of the day.

❷ In general, clouds came with the west wind, from the sea. They brought, of course, the rain. It was for this reason that Elijah was able to announce the coming of rain (I Kings 18:43–45).

❸ The south wind in Palestine (as throughout the Orient) is particularly dreaded. It is the *khamsin* which brings a sultry, oppressive heat, even in regions like Jerusalem whose altitude should preserve them from what is truly a pestilence.

❹ This type of accident is not very well understood in the West, but it is confirmed even today (and to the letter) in the Orient. Daily, children "fall into the fire." The fire burns or smolders unceasingly in the court of the house or in the center of the tent; embers are kept under the ashes in the hearth in order to save on matches. In Jesus' day, matches had not yet been invented, so it was absolutely necessary to keep the fire

1 *Didrachma and stater (Matthew 17:24–27)*

2 *It would be better for him to have a great millstone fastened round his neck (Matthew 18:6; Mark 9:42)*

3 *The lost sheep (Matthew 18:10–14; Luke 15:3–7)*

going. Nearly every week, at the house in our excavation camp, we saw women arrive with their children who had fallen into the fire and who wanted us to try to treat the fresh burns. The epileptic of the Gospel (Mark 9:18, 20; Luke 9:39) fell into the fire, but we are also told that he fell into the water (Matt. 17:15; Mark 9:22). We have no personal memories to help clarify the latter, but perhaps it was into the large jars containing the store of water that he fell. It did not involve the lake, or the rivers, or the *birkets* (pools), so frequent in Hauran, where the village women go to fill their pitchers.

Apparently the scene was still Upper Galilee, after the event of the Transfiguration — if, as we believe, the Transfiguration took place on a slope of Mount Hermon.

❶ Each year, every Jew had to pay a half-shekel (Exod. 30:13) as temple tax. This half-shekel corresponded to the Greek didrachma, which, we are told, was collected at Capernaum. The tax for two persons (Jesus and Peter) was thus four drachmas or one shekel or, again, one stater. It was a stater that was to be found in the mouth of the fish that Peter was sent to catch. Silver money from Tyre was also used in Galilee. On one such coin, dated and inscribed "of the Tyrians," are figured an eagle and a hammer, the symbol of Heracles-Melcarth.

❷ Even today in the villages, one can see an installation that illustrates this text perfectly. A millstone, pierced in the middle in order to accommodate a beam, is turned by an ass hitched to the beam. The ass is blindfolded and tirelessly treads the same circuit. The millstone turns on an enormous circular stone, which is more or less hollowed out, on which is spread whatever needs to be ground (grain or olives). It is easily understood how a man with such a heavy millstone around his neck would quickly sink "to the depth of the sea," whence he would never rise. Luke (17:2), who has included this incident also, mentions only the "millstone" without adding the detail of local color about the asses which turn it.[1]

❸ One hundred sheep are a small fortune, and it is very easy to lose track of one, for the regions of pasturage are quite rough. The plains (such as Sharon, Esdraelon, or Gennesaret) are reserved for crops. Thus the sheep graze on the hills and even on the "mountains." And in order to find its food, the sheep must move about constantly. It

1 [Nor do Matthew and Mark, in the English versions (RSV, NEB).]

1 *Ten thousand talents and a hundred denarii (Matthew 18:23–35)*

2 *He said to Simon, "Put out into the deep and let down your nets for a catch" (Luke 5:4–6)*

3 *Soon afterward he went to a city called Nain. . . . As he drew near to the gate of the city, behold, a man who had died was being carried out, the only son of his mother, and she was a widow (Luke 7:11–15)*

can quickly move out of sight of the shepherd, who often is a young boy. A Bedouin of the Taᶜamireh was seeking a lost sheep in the wilderness of Judea, precisely "on the hills" (Matt. 18:12) and "in the wilderness" (Luke 15:4), when he discovered the first cave of Qumran, with the first "Dead Sea Scrolls."

❶ Jesus chose numbers as different as possible in order to emphasize the contrast between the attitude of the king, who canceled a debt of 10,000 talents which his servant owed him, and that of the servant, who refused to cancel a debt of only 100 denarii which was owed him by a fellow servant. The talent was a weight of gold or

61.   Young shepherd.

silver worth 6000 denarii. In other words, the larger sum was the equivalent of 60 million drachmas, which was a fabulous sum; the smaller sum was only 100 denarii (the Roman equivalent of drachmas).

❷ For the specialist, let us say that the Sea of Galilee abounds in fish of the type *Chromidae*, which is divided into eight species. The most abundant of the *Chromidae* are the *Chromis niloticus* (which weigh up to seven pounds), the *Chromus tiberiadis*, which move about in tightly packed groups, and the *Chromis Simonis*. There are also carp and *alburnus̓ silla*, which look like sardines and are caught by the thousands in the springtime.[1]

❸ The name, if not the exact site, of Nain is conserved in the present Nein, which is not far from Mount Tabor and 5 miles south-southeast of Nazareth. In our time, it is a very small village, but during the time of Jesus it must have been a large town (the text speaks of a "city"). It had a gate, and therefore walls. The dead person was carried on a bier rather than in a coffin; the face was uncovered. Thus Jesus could call to him, "Young man," and the latter could sit up erect (vs. 14).

[1] Information from Abel, *Géographie de la Palestine*, I, p. 231.

1 *Some women were with him (Luke 8:2–3)*

● Luke alone gives the information that the small group made up by Jesus and the disciples was free of material concerns, thanks to the generosity of some women, all of whom evidently were Galileans. Three are designated by name: Mary of Magdala (today, Mejdel, on the shore, a few miles north of Tiberias), "from whom seven demons had gone out" (cf. Luke 8:30; 11:26) and whom some exegetes identify with the "sinner" of Luke 7:37; Joanna, the wife of Chuza, Herod's steward (Herod Antipas, tetrarch of Galilee), who was also present on Easter morning at the empty tomb (Luke 24:10); Susanna, who is mentioned only in this place and who does not reappear later; and several other women who remain anonymous.

Contrary, perhaps, to expectation, the wives of the disciples are not listed among this group. But the reason is simple: the wives of the disciples were not wealthy, and the accent in this passage is on the personal and disinterested contribution of the women. However, other women were in the group, including the mother of the sons of Zebedee (Matt. 20:20). These women were at the foot of the cross (Matt. 27:56; Mark 15:40), and the first two Gospels state explicitly that the Galilean women were present at the time of the Crucifixion (Matt. 27:55; Mark 15:40–41). This is a magnificent example of loyalty at a time when all of the disciples, except one, had disappeared.

The mention of Joanna indicates that the gospel had penetrated even into the interior of the court of Herod Antipas, who must have had some inkling that the wife of his steward had been won over to the movement and had thrown her lot in with a person whom some considered to be seditious. Perhaps this explains why the monarch had desired to know more of Jesus (Luke 9:9).

62. Funeral procession.

63

1 *Authority to tread upon serpents and scorpions (Luke 10:19)*

2 *Now when Jesus had finished these sayings, he went away from Galilee and entered the region of Judea beyond the Jordan (Matthew 19:1; Mark 10:1)*

63. Scorpion.

❶ This verse has a meaning that is even more spiritual than material, but, taken literally, its meaning is clear. For people who almost always walk barefoot and in areas infested with dangerous animals, nothing is more feared than snakes (often of the horned viper species, whose bite is fatal) and scorpions, whose sting is extremely painful. It is a priceless victory to have the certitude of being not only immune but even insensible to attacks of this type. The spiritual aspect is even more of a victory.

❷ There is much controversy concerning this itinerary, for the manuscripts present major variations. Leaving Galilee, Jesus either entered first into Judea and then later went on to the other side of the Jordan, that is, to Perea; or, as we believe, he first started to cross through Samaria but, receiving a rather chilly reception there, took the eastern route, crossing the Jordan perhaps at the ford of ed-Damiyeh. He would then have been in Perea, which also belonged to Herod Antipas. There were many towns and villages there in which to teach and preach (Luke 13:22; Mark 10:1). After an indeterminate time, Jesus and his disciples once again took the western route and, crossing the Jordan, were then in Judea.

IV. Jesus and the Samaritans

1 *And he sent messengers ahead of him, who went and entered a village of the Samaritans, to make ready for him; but the people would not receive him (Luke 9:52–53)*

2 *So he came to a city of Samaria, called Sychar, near the field that Jacob*

❶ In 722 B.C., the Assyrians took Samaria and deported the inhabitants (II Kings 17:6); the prism of Sargon, discovered at Nimrud [Kalah] in 1952, gives the number of deportees as 27,280. The Assyrians then brought in another population from conquered territories (II Kings 17:24). This new population, however, met with a number of misfortunes because of the lions that roamed the province (II Kings 17:25–26) and because of an attempt to bring them into line regarding the proper worship of Yahweh. This did not prevent the new colonists from continuing to worship their national gods. The result was a somewhat syncretistic religion, one rather far removed from the Yahwism that had been reestablished by Ezra. Samaria took on more and more the character of a schismatic state, separated politically and religiously from the rest of the country. The ultimate result was a veritable hostility, and even hate, between the Jews and the Samaritans. Those to whom the messengers of Jesus (probably James and John) had been sent refused purely and simply to accord hospitality to the travelers. Jesus did not insist, and traveled farther along his way, refusing to call down the reprisals that James and John asked for (Luke 9:54–55). Not only did he not share the feelings of his fellow country-men, but, on the contrary, he made a great effort to bring out what was good in the Samaritans. Even more, whenever the opportunity presented itself, he utilized Samaritans as good examples: among ten lepers who were healed, the only one to express thanks was a Samaritan (Luke 17:16); on the Jericho road, neither the priest nor the Levite paused to help the man who had been beaten by robbers, but the Samaritan stopped (Luke 10:33). Only once did Jesus depart from this irenic attitude, when, in giving instructions to his disciples, he said explicitly: "Enter no town of the Samaritans" (Matt. 10:5). This is easily explained: it is useless to court certain failure. The essential thing was to reach first and foremost "the lost sheep of the house of Israel." This is what Jesus had at first replied to the Canaanite woman from the region of Tyre and Sidon (Matt. 15:24). On another occasion, Jesus wanted to show that Samaritans were not unresponsive to conversation, and to this end he spoke with a woman at Jacob's well.

❷ Of all the "holy places" of Palestine, none has more reason to be considered authentic than Jacob's well. Indeed, there is no reason why its authenticity should be questioned. The "field of Jacob" is in the plain, east of Shechem (modern Balatah)

gave to his son Joseph. Jacob's well was there, and so Jesus, wearied as he was with his journey, sat down beside the well. It was about the sixth hour. There came a woman of Samaria to draw water. Jesus said to her, "Give me a drink" (John 4:5–7)

and south of Sychar (modern Askar). In this field, a little over half a mile from the village, there is a well over which a church has been built. The church, originally dating from the 4th century A.D., was reconstructed by the Crusaders and later restored by the Greek Orthodox. Today the well is under a crypt in the middle of a garden. One descends into the crypt by one staircase and ascends by another staircase. A Greek monk offers each visitor a cup of cool and pleasant-tasting water, drawn from a depth of 128 feet. "The well is deep," the Samaritan woman said (John 4:11), much deeper than other wells, where the water comes up almost to the sides. The scene is described with an extraordinary feeling for reality.

It was midday and Jesus was tired. It was not the normal hour for women to come out to draw water (cf. Gen. 24:11); had it been the customary hour, there would not have been *one* woman but a whole line of women, and the conversation would never have taken place. Jesus' disciples had gone to buy provisions, perhaps at Shechem. The Samaritan woman arrived, carrying her jug and cord (since the equipment was too precious to leave by the well, each woman

64. Palestinian woman going to draw water.

65. Plain of Askar.
66. Gerizim and Jacob's well.

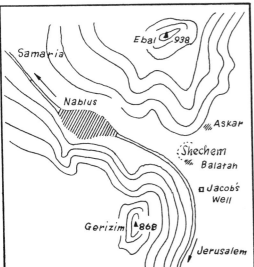

brought her own). Jesus was thirsty. He asked for a little water. And the dialogue began. How was it that he, a Jew, had dared to address a Samaritan woman? Did he not share his countrymen's animosity towards the people of the region? Not only did he not share this animosity, but he in turn offered living water, water which refreshes forever. And when the woman stretched out her arm to point out the eastern slope of Mount Gerizim, where the Samaritans had a sanctuary, rival to that of Jerusalem, Jesus interrupted her: it was neither on that mountain, which both were looking at, nor at Jerusalem, where the temple was, that true worshipers would gather together. Religion in spirit and in truth would no longer know either nations or frontiers. When the disciples returned, they were astonished to see Jesus talking with a woman (vs. 27). In the oriental mentality, a man never addresses himself to a woman unless she is a member of his family. Otherwise he must ignore her.

67. Mt. Gerizim.

68. The Church of the Well of the Samaritan Woman.

1 *A man was going down from Jerusalem to Jericho (Luke 10:30)*

❶ From Jerusalem (2593 ft. above sea level) to Jericho (820 ft. below sea level), the route truly "goes down." The region is well chosen for the setting of a story about robbers and waylaying. Until very recently, many were the travelers who had these "exciting" adventures: you were halted by the bandits, who wanted not only your money but also your clothing and were satisfied only when you were condemned to reach less deserted places in an outfit worthy of our father Adam. We knew a venerable Benedictine father in Jerusalem who was the protagonist in such an incident. But he, at least, returned home in perfect health, without having suffered any blows (except to his dignity). His passive acceptance of the robbery had saved him; the man in the parable had been less docile. Nevertheless, he had still been "stripped," and since, in the East, the present often helps us to understand the past, we should perhaps give full meaning to the term "stripped." Once their evil deed was done, the malefactors disappeared. The priest and the Levite were the first travelers to come by, but neither stopped. A Samaritan then arrived, who took charge of the unfortunate man. First, he dressed the man's wounds with oil and wine. Then he took him to an inn, in order that the man could

69. A man was going down from Jerusalem to Jericho.

V. Jesus in Perea and in Judea

70. The robbers' cave.

be cared for by someone until he was completely healed. But the Samaritan did more: he paid the cost of the man's treatment. Jesus asked the Doctor of the Law which of the three men had proved neighbor to the unfortunate man, and the lawyer could respond in only one way: obviously the heretic, the enemy, the Samaritan, to the shame of the two representatives of the Jewish religion. There are two interesting details in this parable. For one thing, there was the use of wine and oil to dress the wounds. These two products are common provisions of the traveler, who carries them in his saddlebags. Second, there were the two denarii, the wages for two days of work, to pay for the cost of treatment. We do not know if there is some factual incident, especially a generous act of a Samaritan, at the origin of this parable. Even today, on the Jericho road some 12 miles from Jerusalem, guides show the cave where the robbers hid and the "inn" (modern), which has been turned into a police station. It is a fact that this region had an uncertain reputation, for since the Byzantine period there has been some type of military outpost there.

1 *Go and tell that fox (Luke 13:32)*

2 *It is easier for a camel to go through the eye of a needle than for a rich man to enter the kingdom of God (Matthew 19:24; Mark 10:25)*

3 *The laborers of the eleventh hour (Matthew 20:1–16)*

❶ Jesus must still have been in Perea when some Pharisees came to warn him that Herod Antipas wanted to kill him. And Jesus replied to them, "Go and tell that fox. . . ." A fox is a sly but timorous animal who lives in his den and leaves it only after nightfall.

❷ The enormity of the comparison has caused much debate among scholars, and attempts have been made to deal with the obvious difficulties, either by translating the Greek term *kamelos* by "cable," or by imagining a small gate in Jerusalem called "the needle gate." However, the comparison should without doubt be taken literally. Otherwise, the moral would be pointless. Furthermore, how else could one explain the stupefaction of the disciples? It is in exactly the same vein that Jesus utilizes the comparison between the gnat and the camel (Matt. 23:24).

❸ The working day begins at sunup and ends at sundown, in the Orient (at least before the inauguration of the eight-hour working day). The employer thus went out "early in the morning." He found some workers (these are always easy to recruit, since there is an abundance of laborers) and fixed the day's wages. This is indispensable, for trust is always somewhat limited. It is necessary to settle carefully all questions of payment beforehand, in order to avoid interminable disputes when it comes time to settle accounts. The vineyard produces the principal crop of Palestine, which is also the crop requiring the most care. At 9 A.M. there are always plenty of candidates for work. By this time, if they are hired, they are so thankful to have work that they do not haggle about what they will be paid. They know that in any case they will be able to demand a denarius. At midday and even at 3 P.M. there are still some "unemployed," which is normal, since the size of the work force exceeds the demand for workers. But here the text provides a detail drawn from life: those who do not have work quite simply stand about "all day with nothing to do" (vs. 6, NEB). Literally. They do not walk around, nor read, nor "putter about" in an attempt to kill time. As in Jesus' day, so in ours: the man without work squats there rolled up in his cloak, in the sun or sheltered from the wind, and waits without apparent boredom until the coming of night chases him to his home. That the owner of the vineyard hired more workers at the eleventh hour of work (out of a total of twelve hours) is proof of his kindness and generosity. All work stopped at evening (vs. 8). This is an absolute rule.

71

1 *He entered Jericho and was passing through. And there was a man named Zacchaeus; he was a chief tax collector, and rich. And he sought to see who Jesus was, but could not, on account of the crowd, because he was small of stature. So he ran on ahead and climbed up into a sycamore tree (Luke 19:1–4)*

71. Denarius.

One never profits from the last rays of the short twilight period. When the sun has set, each man returns home with his pay, since often one is paid that day for the day's work.

A denarius (worth about twenty cents) is approximately what we give our workers. It is the pay for a day of sweating "the whole day long in the blazing sun" (vs. 12, NEB). All of the details fit, for with the heat, thirst increases the worker's burden. One denarius. The owner of the vineyard gave each of his workers one little silver coin,[1] no matter whether he had worked for one hour or for the whole period from sunup to sundown. This shocks our sense of justice and equity, and it set off a lively argument (vs. 11). However, it is true that the divine

benevolence has nothing in common with human justice. We should not complain.

1 Jesus had now left Perea and the territory of Herod Antipas, and had arrived at Jericho. The city, during the time of Jesus, was not located on the site of the Canaanite or Israelite city. It was situated on the plain to the southwest, at the entrance of Wadi Qelt, at a place now called Tulul Abu el-Alayiq. In recent years a great palace has been uncovered there, probably the winter residence of Herod the Great, later occupied by his son Archelaus. Jericho was the first city of Judea, the territory of the procurator Pilate; thus it was a heavily trafficked frontier city with a major customs station. All merchandise entering the city was subject to quite precise duties. Zacchaeus occupied the preeminent post among the customs officials and tax collectors, since he was "superintendent of taxes" (vs. 2, NEB).

Zacchaeus' curiosity got the better of him, which is an understandable human failing. Who, during the course of his life, has not once or twice stood in a crowd in order to see some great person pass by? But Zacchaeus was short, and since he was not in the front ranks of "rubbernecks," he made the very simple decision to view the proces-

---

[1] About 1930, it was still one silver coin that we paid to the workers on the excavation crews in Syria (one medjidie) and Iraq (one rupee).

1 *As he was leaving Jericho with his disciples and a great multitude, Bartimaeus, a blind beggar, the son of Timaeus, was sitting by the roadside (Mark 10:46)*

2 *Parable of the pounds (Luke 19:12–27)*

sion from the top of a tree. Running on ahead, he climbed a sycamore tree. This is a tree that is often found in the plains and in the oasis of Jericho. It reaches heights of between 26 and 55 feet, with branches spreading out some 65 feet. Thus the sycamore is a perfect observation post. What Zacchaeus had undoubtedly not foreseen, nor even dared to consider, did in fact happen: Jesus noticed him, bade him come down, and followed him into his house.

❶ The Gospels contain minor variations regarding this incident: two blind men are mentioned in Matthew (20:30); in Luke (18:35), the blind man is not named, and the incident takes place not as Jesus leaves, but as he enters the city (from the Jordan side). During that era, a blind man was a miserable being, literally abandoned. He had no trade, and was thus without means of subsistence. The only thing left for him to do was to beg. His only recourse was to incite the passersby to pity, and to do this he had to sit by the side of the road. This seems to have been the rule, since the blind man healed at Siloam did the same (John 9:8). When Bartimaeus learned that Jesus was coming, he rushed forward. The passage includes an excellent detail: in order to move more swiftly, Bartimaeus threw off his mantle. Bartimaeus asked not for money but for sight, in order to become a true man once more and to regain independence — he who was dependent upon all. A new petition, and a new granting of the petition.

❷ Jesus must have "hung" his parable on an historical fact: this nobleman who went into a far country to receive kingly power and then return could well have been Archelaus. On the death of Herod the Great (4 B.C.), his son Archelaus did in fact go to Rome, in order to receive confirmation of his father's will leaving him the territory which included Judea and Samaria. His enemies tried to thwart him by sending their own embassy (to which vs. 14 explicitly alludes), but without success. Before the nobleman departed, he distributed one mina [pound] to each of ten servants. The mina was a Greek unit of weight. It was worth one-sixtieth of a talent and was equivalent to 100 drachmas (about $20). Luke's account is not perfectly coherent: ten servants had received money, but only three were called in on the master's return. Nor does it become immediately apparent what relationship the "enemies" of the king (who reappear in vs. 27) have to the behavior of the more cautious or less cautious servants.

1 *Parable of the talents (Matthew 25:14–30)*

❶ The parable of the talents is quite probably the same parable as that of the pounds, but recounted in a different fashion by Matthew. No motive is given for the journey of the master of the house; he calls only three servants (instead of ten, as in Luke); instead of minas, he gives them respectively five, two, and one talents. The talent was the weight of a certain sum of silver or gold. The silver talent represented 6000 drachmas (about $1200). The servant who received five talents, then, was in possession of a veritable fortune, especially when one considers the higher purchase power of money in the Orient. The first servant had a flair for financial affairs: he doubled his investment. The second had the same gift, and also doubled his investment. The third, more fearful, decided to be simply the guardian of his money; indeed, he did not even have the courage to assume full responsibility for it, since he entrusted his talent to the ground. In Luke's account, the servant hid his mina in a handkerchief, a *sudarium* (a napkin with which one sponged oneself), according to the text. The master returns. The servants render their accounts. The first two could easily have given the master only what they had received and no more, and could have pocketed the profits of their operation. After all, the master would have known nothing about it; since he had given them five and two talents, he would simply have

72. The Mount of Olives.

1 *And they were on the road, going up to Jerusalem, and Jesus was walking ahead of them (Mark 10:32; Matthew 20:17)*

2 *And when they drew near to Jerusalem and came to Bethphage, to the Mount of Olives, then Jesus sent two disciples, saying to them, "Go into the village opposite you" (Matthew 21:1; Mark 11:1; Luke 19:29)*

received back what he had given them. The honesty of the two servants should be emphasized, and yet it was something more than simple honesty. The last servant is called and comes with his one talent, which he has retrieved from its hiding place. The master is angry and immediately punishes the servant: he takes the talent from the lazy servant and drives him out (although it is not explicitly stated, the two zealous servants must have received their reward in being permitted to keep the original sum). To put this in other words, had we received only one gift — a talent — it would still be necessary to make it increase in value, for this gift is really only a loan for which we must render account.

❶ When one returns to Jerusalem via the route from the east, the road makes a continuous and steep ascent. In effect, one must go from 820 feet below sea level to almost 2500 feet above sea level — over a distance of about 19 miles.[1]

❷ So far, it has been impossible to locate the village of Bethphage exactly, and this will become more and more difficult to attempt as construction work extends out on this side of Jerusalem (we were able, in 1965, to take account once again of this

[1] The present road (1965) is about 24 miles long, for it has been made easier.

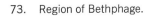

73. Region of Bethphage.

1 *You will find an ass tied, and a colt with her; untie them and bring them to me (Matthew 21:2)*

2 *They brought the ass and the colt, and put their garments on them (Matthew 21:7; Mark 11:7; Luke 19:35)*

growth). Sometimes scholars suggest the small valley which separates the ancient site of Bethany from the modern urban district of Kefr et-Tur, on the summit of the Mount of Olives, because further on there is a steep hill, then the Kidron ravine and Jerusalem. *Bethphage* means "house of unripe figs."

❶ Matthew is alone in speaking of an ass *and* a colt, for Mark (11:2) and Luke (19:30) mention only a colt. The two versions are in no way contradictory. It is

74. She-ass and foal.

obvious that Jesus had need of only one animal and that he was not about to mount two! Once again we are able to cite a specific case, which we observed in 1964. On our excavation at Mari we utilized a she-ass to carry water. That year she had a foal and would not leave it for anything; wherever she went, she was followed by the foal gamboling about her. Couldn't it have been the same in the case of the she-ass of Bethphage?

❷ Even today the donkey is a widely used means of transport in Palestine as well as in Lebanon and Syria. One mounts it without saddle or stirrups, with one's legs hanging down. Sometimes packsaddles are slung over the hindquarters of the animal, with two saddlebags on the sides. The disciples used their cloaks for Jesus to sit upon. It was a solemn and messianic entry, since it fulfilled the prophecy of Zechariah (9:9). It is, perhaps, amazing that a "king" would appear in such a way. One would expect him to arrive on a dashing steed. But the Mari tablets show us that it is not understood in that fashion. The prefect of the palace, Badi-Lim, wrote to the king, Zimri-Lim, that "to honor his royal head," he should by no means mount horseback but travel "solely in a chariot or on mules."

VI. Jesus at Jerusalem

1 *Others cut branches from the trees and spread them on the road (Matthew 21:8; Mark 11:8)*

2 *And when he drew near and saw the city he wept over it (Luke 19:41)*

75. General view of Jerusalem.

❶ The branches could have been cut from olive, fig, or palm trees (John 12:13). The detail of the cloaks being thrown onto the road as the procession passed accentuates even more the honor that was paid to Jesus. In a time less remote, we have seen a Near Eastern king (who has since disappeared) advancing on a pathway strewn with rose petals. At Jerusalem the route was covered with branches.

❷ The procession had passed by the Mount of Olives and had begun to descend toward Jerusalem. It was then that the Holy City appeared, with the white blanket of its houses. In the foreground was the Haram and its enceinte, today the Mosque of Abd al-Malik (wrongly called the Mosque of Omar), formerly the site of the temple of Herod the Great. Ever since the 14th century, the place where Jesus wept (today the Franciscan Chapel of Dominus Flevit) has been pointed out. But there is some doubt about this location. The slope is direct and too steep for a procession like that of Palm Sunday, and would not have accommodated a crowd of the type that is reported in the Gospels. Thus it seems preferable to presuppose a more southerly route, one which would follow the con-

1 The merchants of the temple (Matthew 21:12; Mark 11:15; Luke 19:45; John 2:14–16)

76. General view of Bethany. (Photograph taken in 1928; in 1965, the region was unrecognizable.)

tours of the hills and descend a much gentler slope. Modern constructions and an imposing asphalt road have unfortunately hidden everything from view. The cloister walls of religious estates add to this, and make impossible any general view.

❶ Merchants and money changers were installed on the vast esplanade of the Herodian temple (1575 ft. at the west, 985 ft. at the north), under the porticoes, and in the Court of the Gentiles. The merchants sold animals destined for use in sacrifices: cattle, sheep, and pigeons, the latter being offerings of the poor (Lev. 12:8; Luke 2:24). The money changers, sitting behind their counters, provided Jewish money to those who had only foreign money (Greek or Roman). We have encountered latter-day descendents of these shrewd persons, seated behind small glass chests containing Greek drachmas, silver Turkish medjidies

1 *And leaving them, he went out of the city to Bethany and lodged there (Matthew 21:17)*

and gold Turkish pounds, Syrian piastres, and Iraqi rupees. It is not at all surprising that the merchants and money changers were "robbers" (Matt. 21:13; Mark 11:17). In the Orient, in the past as now, commerce (such as it is) has always been carried on with a good dose of larceny. It is somewhat better now with the increasingly general acceptance of the "fixed price."

❶ Bethany is only 15 stadia from Jerusalem (John 11:18), or just under 2 miles. The walk is not long, but it is tiring if one walks too fast and if one takes the short route. The road from the temple to the Kidron is steep; it goes up along the western slope of the Mount of Olives, then dips down again and finally climbs up once more, arriving finally at Bethany.

At the site of the old village, there are only a few olive trees and some cisterns where the women still come to draw water. The modern village, el-Azariyeh, further down, is grouped around the "tomb of Lazarus," on which a church has stood since the 4th century (it was transformed into a mosque in the 16th century). To the west, there is the ruined wall of a Benedictine abbey built in the 12th century by Queen Millicent. Excavations carried out from 1949 to 1953 by the Franciscan fathers, in lands that be-

77. Woman drawing water at Bethany.

1 *The vineyard (Matthew 21:28, 33–41; Mark 12:1–9; Luke 20:9–16)*
2 *The parable of the marriage feast (Matthew 22:2–14; Luke 14:16–24)*

longed to them and that adjoined the "tomb," uncovered the remains of four churches, all dedicated to the remembrance of the Gospel event and ranging from the 4th century to the 12th century. Also in Bethany, on the lands belonging to the Daughters of Charity, excavations in 1950 disclosed a cave-cistern, decorated with Christian emblems, which Father Benoit believed to be the cistern that was shown to pilgrims in the 9th century as the place where Lazarus had gone to wash himself after his resurrection. In any event, it has been established that this site was the object of an intense and prolonged veneration of pilgrims during the first centuries of the Christian Era.

❶ The vines are the most important agricultural item; they are not tall and straight shoots, but stocks that creep on the ground.

78.   Tower in a vineyard.

When the harvest is ready, the stocks are raised up with a piece of wood so that the bunches will not drag on the ground and be spoiled.

The parable of the "wicked husbandmen" is notable for local color. After the planting, the vineyard is closed off, either by means of a wall of dry stones or, just as good, a hedge of cactus (prickly pears), which provides both a screen and a solid barrier. The winepress (or the vat) is fitted out in the ground. It is, briefly, a pit lined with hastily cemented rocks or a vat cut into the rocks. As for the "tower," this was a circular dry-stone construction in which was sheltered and hidden the guardian hired to watch over the property: during the fruit season the danger of theft increased. One could add a few dogs, and the picture would be complete.

❷ Even today, in the Orient, it is the supreme affront to refuse an invitation, especially when it comes from a person of high rank. The preparations for the banquet were long and complicated: the "oxen and fat calves" were the essential things, but there were many accessories. After the first invited guests failed to respond, a second round of guests was solicited. These were

1 *Render therefore to Caesar the things that are Caesar's, and to God the things that are God's (Matthew 22:17–21; Mark 12:14–17; Luke 20:21–25)*

2 *The scribes and the Pharisees sit on Moses' seat (Matthew 23:2)*

3 *They bind heavy burdens, hard to bear . . . ; but they themselves will not move them with their finger (Matthew 23:4)*

not the cream of the population, and it was not difficult to recruit them. The thoroughfares and the streets are always full of vagrants. These people accepted willingly. However, this acceptance had to be accompanied by the proper gesture: over the rags and tatters, one had to wear one's best holiday robe. To do otherwise would be to mock the host who welcomes you. Even today, upon our arrival or upon our departure, or on paydays (which are preeminently our at-home days), our Bedouin workers appear only after first having donned the proper cloak, a new *keffiyeh* or a white *chemise*. These are gestures of honor and reverence. When one knows and remembers Eastern politeness and its nuances, one is not surprised that the king ejected one of his guests who had neglected this elementary duty.

❶ The state tax was owed by every inhabitant of the Roman province, and thus by the residents of Judea, the land of a procurator. The tax was one silver denarius, the salary for one day's work (cf. Matt. 20:2). Jesus called for a coin and asked the question: "Whose likeness and inscription is this?" The likeness in this case was that of Tiberius, represented in left profile with the inscription around it: "Tiberius Caesar, son of the divine Augustus, Augustus." On the obverse, Pax is seated upon her throne, holding a palm branch in her left hand. Inscribed around the figure of Pax are the words *Pontif(ex) maxim(us)*. The Romans alone had the right to strike silver money. The Jews utilized the Roman money without too many scruples despite the fact that their Law prohibited representations. Once again, Jesus foiled an insidious question. At the same time, he clearly marked the separation between what belongs to the state and what belongs to God and underlined the distinction between the two domains.

❷ Often it is thought that this passage is only metaphorical, signifying that the task of the scribes and the Pharisees is to teach or to apply the Mosaic laws. In reality, the text should be taken literally. In effect, the synagogue contained a chair reserved for the preacher of the Law. One such chair, in basaltic stone, has recently been discovered in the ruins of the synagogue of Chorazin. The chair is decorated and is inscribed with the name of a certain Yudan, son of Ishmael.[1]

❸ This image is undoubtedly taken from daily life. The poor and the lower classes carried enormous loads on their backs. The

[1] A photograph may be seen in *Views of the Biblical World*, 5, *The New Testament*, p. 63.

1 *They make their phylacteries broad and their fringes long (Matthew 23:5)*
2 *You shut the kingdom of heaven against men (Matthew 23:13)*
3 *"If any one swears by the gold of the temple, he is bound by his oath" (Matthew 23:16)*
4 *He . . . swears by the throne of God (Matthew 23:22)*

scribes and the Pharisees, for their part, thought it dishonorable to be seen in the streets carrying even a miniscule package. This same prejudice still exists in the Orient, where the streets are alive with a swarm of porters waiting and watching for the chance to carry someone's load.

❶ Phylacteries are pieces of parchment enclosed in small boxes; they are attached to leather straps, by which they are fastened to the left arm and to the center of the forehead before prayer. On the parchment are written extracts from the Old Testament (Exod. 13:1–10, 11–16; Deut. 6:4–9; 11:13–21). Several phylacteries have been discovered in recent years near the Dead Sea, both at Murabbaat and in the caves at Qumran. The fringes of which Jesus speaks

79. Lock from Sur Baher.

were prescribed in Numbers (15:38–39), to serve as a sign and a reminder of the commandments of Yahweh.

❷ This is of course a figure of speech, but it is based on something quite real. Those who have no idea of what a lock was like during the time of Jesus may always see, in the Louvre, a bronze mechanism coming from Sur Baher. It is a rather primitive bolting-mechanism, but effective.

❸ Jesus had said not to swear at all (Matt. 5:34–35). In this, he was going counter to an inveterate, solidly established custom. The oath taken on "the gold of the temple" reminds us of the bronze plaques found in 1952 in Cave 3 at Qumran. The text found on these plaques gave the list of hiding places, from Gerizim to Hebron, where a fabulous treasure was supposedly hidden. For those who, like us, believe that this is not a copyist's fantasy but a real reference to buried treasure, two hypotheses can be formulated: either the fortune is that of the Jewish state, or it is that of the temple. The total sum represents some two hundred tons of gold or silver. In any event, to swear "by the gold of the temple" was no small thing.

❹ The Sumerian gods were generally seated; the Assyrian gods were erect on

1 *You blind guides, straining out a gnat and swallowing a camel! (Matthew 23:24)*

2 *You cleanse the outside of the cup and of the plate (Matthew 23:25)*

3 *You are like whitewashed tombs (Matthew 23:27)*

various beasts, their symbolical animals (Isa. 46:1 probably alludes to this); the Phoenicians frequently sculpted empty thrones, reserved for their deities. As far as the Israelites were concerned, although all representation of Yahweh was forbidden, they nevertheless "imagined" him. Their expression was: "enthroned upon the cherubim" (Ps. 80:1), that is, seated upon a throne beside which stood winged animals with human heads (so Ahiram, king of Byblos, on his sarcophagus).

❶ A piece of cloth is often placed over the vessel containing the water provisions in order to keep dust, flies, and mosquitoes out. In the Orient, whoever says "water" generally says immediately "mosquitoes." The parable of the "gnat" and the camel is a striking example. If it were necessary, this passage would prove that Matthew 19:24 is to be taken literally. The camel is as difficult to "swallow" as the "eye of a needle" or the "log in the eye" (Matt. 7:3). These images are used deliberately. If we forget this, we risk misunderstanding the teaching of Jesus.

❷ The rabbinical prescriptions regarding purity and impurity (Lev. 11–15) had become so complicated that a man found himself enclosed in a network of obligations and prohibitions, and life became thereby one long series of matters of conscience. In the area of observances, the Pharisees were unequaled, but Jesus denounced their hypocrisy. Before eating, not only did they wash their hands (Mark 7:3) but also their utensils, that is, the cup and plate. However, this was misleading, because (perhaps to save time) they washed only the outside of the utensil, which their lips or hands would touch. Cups and plates were made either of clay or of metal.

❸ Even today, Muslims annually rewhitewash the tombs of their cemeteries with wide strokes of brushes dipped in a lime mixture. They do this just before the great religious festivals. The Jews had already adopted this practice, and still do it.

80.   "Whitewashed tombs."

1 *You build the tombs of the prophets and adorn the monuments of the righteous (Matthew 23:29)*

The funerary monuments were very modest constructions in the form of parallelepipeds. After a season, one could see the disjointed stones and the cracked masonry. After the whitewashing, the whole thing took on a different appearance, even a new look. One forgot that the tombs covered "dead men's bones and all uncleanness."

❶ Even today, in a suburb north of Jerusalem, about thirty minutes' walk from the Damascus Gate, one is shown a group of tombs called the Tomb of the Judges. The triangular pediment (Fig. 81) is decorated with acanthus. The construction dates, at the earliest, from the end of the Hellenistic period (2nd century B.C.). In the Kidron Valley, dating from the same period, are tombs which bear the names (from north to south) of Jehoshaphat, Absalom, Saint James, and Zechariah. All of these attributions are indefensible. It seems that only Zechariah can be connected with these tombs with any justification. It may be that it was to these "adorned" tombs that Jesus referred when he addressed himself to the scribes and Pharisees in the temple.[1]

81. Tomb of the Judges.

82. Tombs reputed to be those of Absalom, Saint James, and Zechariah.

[1] For these tombs, see our *Golgotha et Saint-Sépulcre* (Neuchâtel: Delachaux et Niestlé), pp. 62–71.

84

1 *Zechariah the son of Barachiah, whom you murdered between the sanctuary and the altar (Matthew 23:35)*

2 *Jesus left the temple and was going away, when his disciples came to point out to him the buildings of the temple. But he answered them, "You see all these, do you not? Truly, I say to you, there will not be left here one stone upon another, that will not be thrown down" (Matthew 24:1–2; Mark 13:1–2; Luke 21:5–6)*

❶ In Herod's temple, the altar was located in the Court of the Priests, about 12 yards from the door of the sanctuary. Thus the site of Zechariah's murder is quite precisely located.

❷ Today one cannot with any degree of certainty identify anything from any of the three temples in the edifice which presently stands on the site of the threshing-floor of Ornan the Jebusite [I Chron. 21:22; II Sam. 24:18]. However, one can distinguish some foundations of the Herodian buildings, the very buildings which Jesus saw and which provoked the admiration of his disciples. The enormous blocks of this period are of a characteristic size, with embossments and cuts that enable one to attribute them without hesitation to the temple of the New Testament period. For example, these foundations can be seen in the substructure of the terrace, on the east, south, and west sides. The stones are anywhere between 5 and 13 yards in length, with a minimum height of 3¼ feet. The "Wailing Wall,"[1] to the west, is part of the Herodian construction. All of the upper buildings were destroyed during the two Jewish revolts, in A.D. 70 and 132.

[1] See our *Le Temple de Jérusalem*, Pl. VI.

83.   The Wailing Wall in Jerusalem.

1 *As he sat on the Mount of Olives opposite the temple (Mark 13:3; Matthew 24:3)*

2 *There will be earthquakes in various places (Mark 13:8)*

3 *When you see the desolating sacrilege set up where it ought not to be (Mark 13:14; Matthew 24:15)*

❶ From the Mount of Olives, one always has the best view of Jerusalem, of the sacred Haram, of the belltowers, the minarets, the terraces of the houses and monasteries. At the hour when the sun goes down, it seems that for a few minutes the light returns, as if the earth had been gathering it in during the day and now were giving back a part of it. Outlined against the peaceful sky are the loopholes of the old ramparts. The walls themselves form a broken belt, for the city is spreading out, largely toward the west and the north. The belltowers announce the end of day, the muezzins (before the era of loudspeakers) on the minarets cry out loudly the signal for the fourth prayer of the day. On the road, the peasants hasten toward their village. Today, the road carries a long line of cars.

❷ Earthquakes are frequent in Palestine and one need only read the Old Testament with a little care to see that tellurian catastrophes are not lacking in the accounts (Isa. 13:13; 24:19; Ezek. 38:20; Amos 1:1; Zech. 14:5). According to Josephus, there was an earthquake in 31 B.C. Roland de Vaux has shown that there very probably was an earthquake at Khirbet Qumran; one effect of it was that the staircase in one of the large underground cisterns was dislocated. There were others as well: in A.D. 551, 748, 808, 1016, 1202, 1837. There was one in 1903, and one on July 11, 1927 whose shock waves we felt in Syria. Nablus, Lydda, and Es-Salt were damaged. At Jerusalem, the cupola of the Holy Sepulcher and the minarets of the Haram; on the Mount of Olives, all of the buildings, the mosque, the Russian Tower, the residences, the Church of the Pater — all were cracked, if not demolished. "The beginning of the sufferings."

❸ This expression, borrowed from Daniel (9:27), predicted a profanation, in that case, the profanation of which Antiochus Epiphanes was guilty when he erected a pagan altar in the temple of Jerusalem. Judas Maccabeus removed it in 165 B.C. and each year, on the feast of the Dedication (Dec. 25), this purification was commemorated (John 10:22). Beginning with this date, the Jews found themselves having to fight on several occasions against similar profanations by the Roman occupiers: the worship of the standards of the legions, the erection of a golden eagle by Herod. After the death of Jesus, there was the attempt of the emperor Caligula to place a statue of himself in the temple. But above all, in A.D. 70, after the fall of Jerusalem, there was the entry of the Roman soldiers into the Holy of Holies. The prophecy of Jesus was then fully realized.

86

1 *Let those who are in Judea flee to the mountains (Matthew 24:16)*

2 *Let him who is on the housetop not go down to take what is in his house (Matthew 24:17; Mark 13:15)*

3 *Let him who is in the field not turn back to take his mantle (Matthew 24:18; Mark 13:16)*

❶ The mountains would be those to the south and southwest of Jerusalem, where one rapidly finds oneself in deserted places. The region ranges from around 500 feet to 1100 feet above sea level. They are undoubtedly small "mountains," but they make a greater impression here than they would elsewhere, for to the east one has the Dead Sea, some 435 feet below sea level. It is impressive, in this respect, to recall the letter from Simeon ben Kosebah (Bar Cochba), the leader of the second Jewish rebellion. The letter, which was found in 1952 in one of the caves of Murabbaat, was addressed to a Yeshua ben Gilgola, the commandant of the outpost. It urged him to take a more severe attitude regarding certain "Galileans." Even if these Galileans were not "Christians," no one can argue that they had not, at the time of danger, followed to the letter the advice which Jesus had given just a century or so before.

❷ The rooftops of the houses of Palestinian villages were (and still are) slightly inclined. This is for the purpose of running off the winter rain into the cisterns, which fortunately were not all broken (Jer. 2:13)! Life is spent on the rooftop, just as Western man spends a great deal of time in his yard. The rooftop is reached by means of an outside staircase. Jesus' meaning in this passage is not entirely clear: either he is suggesting that one remain on the roof rather than seek to shelter himself in the interior; or, as we believe, he is advising that one escape posthaste, since the danger would be so great that one would not have time to gather up one's possessions from inside the house.

❸ The mantle is the second piece of clothing of the men. It is made of camel-skin or sheep's wool, and protects from both sun and rain. One wraps up in it at night to protect oneself from the cold. Mosaic and Jewish law required the creditor who had taken a mantle as security to return it to his debtor at sundown (Exod. 22:27).

84. The mantle.

1 *Pray that your flight may not be in winter (Matthew 24:20; Mark 13:18) or on a sabbath (Matthew 24:20)*

2 *If they say to you, "Lo, he is in the wilderness," do not go out (Matthew 24:26)*

3 *Wherever the body is, there the eagles will be gathered together (Matthew 24:28)*

4 *The sun will be darkened, and the moon will not give its light, and the stars will fall from heaven (Matthew 24:29; Mark 13:24–25; Luke 21:25)*

❶ In the Orient, winter is a gloomy and harsh season. Houses are well enough designed for the heat, but not at all for the cold or for the rain. Then, also, there are the pathways, the outskirts, the country, which the rain turns into a swamp in which one gets bogged down, be it on foot, on horseback, or, as today, in cars. Consequently, because of the rain, one leaves the house as little as possible during the winter. Life comes to a standstill, traffic slows down, everybody awaits the return of the sun. Since the great day would be the signal for flight, it is easy to understand why it was preferable that it not come "in winter."

. . . Or, for that matter, "on a sabbath," because of the sabbath law, which forbade one to journey more than a thousand yards on that day (cf. Acts 1:12).

❷ The wilderness in question is that of Judea, around Jericho or in the hill country south of Jerusalem. It is a wild desert of arid and bare gorges, the haunt of bandits, the refuge of hunted men, the retreat of the hard-pressed.

❸ In the land of Sumer, two and a half millennia before Christ, Eannatum, king of Lagash, raised a stele to commemorate his victory over the neighboring city of Umma. Among other scenes, the stele includes one of a slaughter: a cloud of vultures is carrying off the heads of the vanquished enemy. Indeed, in the Orient, quite often vultures or eagles serve as "gravediggers." And they bring a great activity to this dismal task. Let an ass or a camel be lost on a desert path, and in a few hours the body is torn to shreds, leaving only the skeleton to bleach in the sun: a signpost of a new type, well known and appreciated by the caravans. The vultures gather and do their work by day, and all the faster because at night there are other "enthusiasts," the wolves and the jackals.

❹ Sun, moon, stars—the luminaries which most awed the ancients and which, from the beginning of time, exercised an important function in their life: the sun, whose unexpected eclipses they observed terror-stricken; the moon, with its regular phases, lighting the desert trails; the stars, guides for caravans and portents of human destinies. These lanterns of the sky were divinized. It is these that one sees on the *kudurrus* (cassiterite landmarks from the 13th — 12th centuries B.C.), which were decorated with a whole pantheon.

1 *Then two men will be in the field; one is taken and one is left. Two women will be grinding at the mill; one is taken and one is left (Matthew 24:40–41)*

2 *If the householder had known in what part of the night the thief was coming (Matthew 24:43)*

85. Sun, moon, stars.

❶ The men were responsible for field-work (although today, at least, women help them in the fields); women alone were responsible for the household tasks, that is, the preparation of the meals, the making of bread, the drawing of water. It was the women who handled the mill, either to crush the grain or to press the olives. Thus there was a clear division of duties. When the blind Samson was held in the prison at Gaza, the Philistines, in order to mock him, forced him to work the mill . . . a woman's work (Judg. 16:21). Thus he should be represented at this work, and not turning a great stone twice his size (as we are shown in the staging of the third act of the opera *Samson et Dalila!*).

❷ The Romans divided the night into four "watches" (Matt. 14:25) which corresponded to the following times: the first was between sundown and 9 P.M.; the second between 9 P.M. and midnight; the third between midnight and 3 A.M.; the fourth between 3 A.M. and sunrise. This is the same division which we find in Mark 13:35, characterized in this way: in the evening, at midnight, at cockcrow, in the morning. The Jews, on the contrary, distinguished only three periods, to which Luke 12:38 seems to refer: the first was between sundown and 10 P.M.; the second between 10 P.M. and 2 A.M.; the third between 2 A.M. and sunrise. The thief, quite naturally, operates during the night, since he counts on the darkness to hide his activities better. This is all the more necessary since he must break in, that is, operate outside the house.

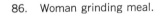

86. Woman grinding meal.

89

1 *The wise and foolish maidens (Matthew 25:1–12)*

2 *He will separate them one from another as a shepherd separates the sheep from the goats, and he will place the sheep at his right hand, but the goats at the left (Matthew 25:32–33)*

3 *I was hungry and you gave me food, I was thirsty and you gave me drink (Matthew 25:35)*

87.   Sheep and goats at pasture.

2 Such a separation is simple, since the sheep are of a beige color and the goats are jet-black. This mixing of the black goats with the sheep is characteristic of Palestinian flocks. The "sheep" would be separated to the right, the noble side, the side of election; the "goats," to the left, which foretold an unhappy fate for them. Indeed, the former were blessed of the Father; the latter, condemned to the eternal fire. The elect and the damned at the Day of Judgment — a subject abundantly treated on the portals of medieval churches.

1 Five maidens were "wise," for they brought a supply of oil in "flasks." The Jewish lamp, in fact, has such a small well that it cannot burn very long without being replenished. Because the bridegroom was delayed, more oil was needed than had been anticipated. When the bridegroom came, the "foolish" hastened away to buy more oil, since their lamps were on the point of going out. The night was already well advanced and, since all of the shops closed at sundown, they had to rouse the shopkeeper. When the maidens returned, the bridegroom had already gone into the "marriage hall" where the banquet was being held. The door had been shut, and it remained shut.

3 At the tribunal of Osiris, the deceased justified themselves in the same fashion and with a very similar formula, for besides the "negative confession" there was also a "positive confession": "I live in the truth, I have reconciled myself to God by my love, I have given bread to the hungry, water to the thirsty, clothing to the naked." The list in the Gospel is more complete, but it is the same theme. The final retribution: eternal happiness or endless fire, heaven or hell, life or death. This is almost "salvation by works," but there is the important qualification that these works are done, in the final analysis, without one's realizing it and without one's having premeditated it.

90

1 *And he sat down opposite the treasury, and watched the multitude putting money into the treasury. . . . And a poor widow came, and put in two copper coins, which make a penny (Mark 12:41–42)*

2 *And he would not allow any one to carry anything through the temple (Mark 11:16)*

3 *Whoever says to this mountain, "Be taken up and cast into the sea" (Mark 11:23)*

4 *The anointing at Bethany (Matthew 26:6–13; Mark 14:3–9; John 12:1–8)*

❶ In the Court of Women (to which men, however, had access), there were thirteen treasuries, in the form of inverted trumpets, which were intended to receive offerings for the needs of the cult. Some were set apart for special offerings (birds, wood, incense, propitiation); others were not. The widow put in two *leptons*, which together made one *quadrans*, that is to say, one quarter of an *as* (or again, one twelfth of a silver *denarius*). The lepton was the smallest of the bronze coins in use in Palestine, and weighed 1½ grams. In order not to go against the Jewish law, the lepton did not have the profile of the emperor; rather, it was ornamented with some approved image, such as that of a palm or a ritual utensil. Perhaps on one side there would be an anchor, and on the other side, a six-pointed star enclosed within a circle of dots. It also would have the title of Caesar and the name of Julia, the mother of the emperor.

❷ The Court of the Gentiles had become a passageway, for it was easy to cross it from east to west or from north to south in order to avoid having to make a longer walk by going around the temple. Consequently, it had become a completely profane route of traffic.

❸ Taking into account the place where these words were uttered, the mountain would be the Mount of Olives and the sea would be the Dead Sea (about 25 miles southeast as the crow flies).

❹ This scene took place at Bethany, in the house of Simon the Leper (Matthew and Mark; John gives no details). A woman approached Jesus (Matthew and Mark do not name her; John says, simply, Mary), with an alabaster jar in her hand. This jar was a simple container, of translucent white stone, containing perfume. The woman poured it out over Jesus' head (Matthew), by breaking the jar (probably at the neck), which was apparently closed (Mark). She did this either to permit the perfume to flow more rapidly or in order to show that the offering was total — contents and container. John says that Mary anointed Jesus' feet

88.   Perfume vase and saucer.

1 *The anointing by the woman who was a sinner (Luke 7:36–50)*
2 *The Lord's Prayer (Matthew 6:9–13; Luke 11:2–4)*
3 *Are not five sparrows sold for two pennies? (Luke 12:6; Matthew 10:29)*

and wiped them with her hair. This is an obvious prefiguration of the rite which would have to be done some days later at Jesus' tomb. The perfume, made of exotic, imported essences, was "very costly." Mark and John tell us that it was worth three hundred denarii. Nothing was too precious for the dinner guest.

❶ This is the identical scene, but in a different context. It apparently took place in Galilee, at the home of a Pharisee who was also called Simon. A woman who was a sinner arrived. She also brought an alabaster jar containing perfume. Weeping profusely, undoubtedly in repentance, her tears wet Jesus' feet, which she then dried with her hair and anointed with the perfume. This series of events is perfectly explainable and, even if Jesus had not explained them later (vss. 44–46), we would easily have understood them. The woman began by washing Jesus' dusty feet with her tears; she dried them with her hair; then, after having kissed them, she anointed them. At Bethany, the ointment was applied with the hair. Here, more respectful and just as loving (which is signified by the kisses), she focuses her attention on the feet. Was it not written: "How beautiful upon the mountains are the feet of him who brings good tidings" (Isa.

52:7)? Did not Jesus also bring *the* good news? We will leave it to the exegetes to be concerned with debating the question of whether or not there were two anointings, with Luke having made use of a tradition different from that used by the other three Evangelists.

❷ There are two opposing traditions concerning the place where Jesus gave the Lord's Prayer to his disciples. According to Matthew, it seems to have been done in Galilee. According to Luke, on the other hand, it must have been in Judea, not far from Jerusalem, since it comes right after the pericope (10:38–42) concerning the village of Martha and Mary (Bethany). One tradition, which goes back only to the Middle Ages, maintains that the Lord's Prayer was given on the western slope of the Mount of Olives, where the Convent of the Pater stands today. No certainty seems to be possible on this point.

❸ The *as* was the smallest copper Roman coin in circulation in Palestine. According to Luke, five sparrows could be bought for two *as*, but in Matthew the price differs somewhat, since according to this Evangelist two sparrows could be purchased for one *as*, hence a higher price. We in the

1 *There were some present at that very time who told him of the Galileans whose blood Pilate had mingled with their sacrifices (Luke 13:1)*

2 *Those eighteen upon whom the tower in Siloam fell (Luke 13:4)*

West undoubtedly would not think of trading in sparrows, but in the Orient, what are called "fig-beaks" are hunted and constitute a very tasty dish.

❶ We do not know what event is alluded to. The Evangelist Luke is the only one to mention it, but it accords perfectly with what we know from other sources concerning Pilate's methods of governing.

❷ Once again, an event which only Luke records and which is not known from extra-biblical sources. It is undoubtedly a matter involving a tower near the canal works

89. Ruins of the Tower of Siloam.

90. Village of Siloam.

1 *Does not each of you on the sabbath untie his ox or his ass from the manger, and lead it away to water it? (Luke 13:15)*

2 *For which of you, desiring to build a tower, does not first sit down and count the cost, whether he has enough to complete it? (Luke 14:28–30)*

which brought water from the spring of Gihon (today, Um ed-Daradj) to the pool of Siloam. These canal works were cut into the hillside, partly under rock and partly open to the sky (Isaiah refers to this as "the waters of Shiloah that flow gently" [8:6]). Excavations have revealed the lower foundations of a circular tower which overlooks this hydraulic installation; perhaps this is the tower spoken of by the Evangelist.

❶ The ox and the ass were the two most common animals; each peasant had them in his stable. These animals are mentioned in the Ten Commandments (Exod. 20:17), and Deuteronomy mentions them explicitly (5:14, 21). At a later date, tradition places an ox and an ass in the manger at Bethlehem, thereby adding to Luke's account, which speaks only of the manger (2:12, 16). The ox drew the plow, the ass served to carry freight.

❷ The tower of Jesus' parable is undoubtedly the small construction that one built in a field, for example, in the middle of the vineyard, in order to provide better surveillance at harvest. When one has lived

91. Pool of Siloam.

1 *The lost coin (Luke 15:8–9)*

2 *The prodigal son (Luke 15:11–32)*

in the Orient, this parable is more easily understood: there is no lack of houses that remain unfinished for the reason indicated. Only the first floor is completed; the preparations for the second story are there, waiting for the next step, which never comes. Houses are not the only buildings left unfinished; sometimes churches, also, like that of the Samaritan at Jacob's well, where the nave continues to await the roof.

92.   Unfinished house.

❶   Ten drachmas is not a great fortune. To lose one drachma was undoubtedly not a catastrophe, but its actual value can be estimated only in relation to the situation. That is to say, one drachma meant much to the woman of the parable. She lit a lamp (it does not say that it was night) because even by day the house, windowless and lighted only through the door, was dark. Thus it was necessary to have more light, and the wick dipped in the oil would provide a little illumination. At last, and not without some effort, the drachma was found and the whole household rejoiced. We should add that the color of the coin, a bronze which easily oxidizes, did not make the search any easier.

❷   This parable is situated only partially in Palestine, since the younger son went "into a far country." If it was a foreign land, it could only have been an adjoining country. A famine arose, an occurrence which is not rare (Gen. 26:1; 41:57; Ruth 1:1; II Sam. 21:1; I Kings 18:2; II Kings 4:38; etc.). Once again it was the peasants who were least affected. The prodigal son, his wealth exhausted, hired himself out to an inhabitant who sent him to take care of his pigs. No occupation could be more humiliating for a Jew, since according to the

95

1 *What shall I do? . . . I am ashamed to beg (Luke 16:3)*
2 *The rich man and Lazarus (Luke 16:19–31)*

Law the pig was unclean. The herd fed on carob, the pods of a plant (*Ceratonia siliqua*) which is found on Cyprus, in Lebanon, and in Asia Minor. It was animal fodder, but men could also eat it if necessary.

After giving his situation some thought, the son decided to return to his own home in order to beg his father's pardon. Everyone knows how he was received: the best robe, shoes on his feet, a ring on his hand (the rich during this time often wore rings, frequently an intaglio of carnelian, set in a gold mounting), and then a banquet, with music and dancing. Engravers and sculptors of antiquity quite often pictured the theme of meals followed by dancing.

1 The greatest disgrace was attached to begging. Only the blind were reduced to this, since they were abandoned by society and yet had to eat in order to live. Such was the case with Bartimaeus, along the Jericho road (18:35). The unfaithful steward had found another system: to make friends for himself "by means of unrighteous mammon." Jesus certainly does not praise him for his conduct, but for his prudence, which is quite a different thing. This parable also informs us that the "rich man" did not manage his fortune himself. Rich men had stewards, that is to say, financial managers. Oriental antiquity provides ample evidence that these stewards constituted a very important class. Their influence was great wherever it was exercised. The Mari archives contain references to many stewards who were attached to the palace.

2 This parable does not speak of actual persons. Lazarus, in particular, is certainly not the brother of Martha and Mary of Bethany. Sometimes excavations discover fragments of cloth, especially in some of the tombs which have been cleared. The evil rich man dressed himself in purple and fine linen; the purple undoubtedly came from Phoenicia, the region of Tyre and Sidon. In the other world Lazarus was in the bosom of Abraham (of which there are exceptionally fine representations on the portals of Moissac and of St. Trophime at Arles); the rich man, suffering in the flames, called out to Abraham to send Lazarus "to dip the end of his finger in water and cool my tongue." Here we find expression of the belief that the deceased, in the realm of the dead, have need of being "refreshed."[1] This belief has such a staying power that, in our

[1] We have studied this question in our *Refrigerium dans l'au-delà* (Paris: Geuthner).

days, the Catholic liturgy requests the *refrigerium* or the *refrigerii sedem* for those who have gone beyond. Originally, this was a cool drink meant to quench their thirst.

❶ Two men *went up* into the temple to pray. During the time of Jesus, the city of Jerusalem was south and southwest of the temple. On the southern side, there was a very steep slope, which Jesus has perfectly rendered with the term he uses. So also when, at the end of the story, he says that the man *went down* to his house.

The scene takes place in the temple, probably in the Court of Israel. The Pharisee is standing, which was the normal attitude in praying (in ancient Mesopotamia, one prayed with the hands folded; one stood, sat, or, more rarely, knelt on one knee). He made a show of his "merits": fasting twice a week (that is, on Monday and Thursday); tithing all his income, which was more than demanded, since normally only certain revenues were taxed. In displaying thus his virtues, the Pharisee probably was facing the altar and the entrance to the sanctuary. The tax collector was standing "far off." Jesus does not say exactly where, but it was within the Court of Israel. We can imagine that he was standing apart, in some corner not far from one of the doors, yet where the Pharisee could see him (vs. 11). The two attitudes are opposed; the final reward was also totally opposed to what one would have expected. Once again, a call for humility.

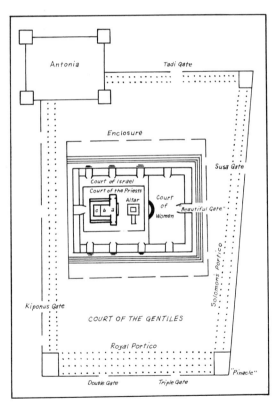

93. Herod's Temple, Jerusalem.

1 *Look at the fig tree, and all the trees; as soon as they come out in leaf, you see for yourselves and know that the summer is already near (Luke 21:29–30)*

2 *Take heed to yourselves lest . . . that day come upon you suddenly like a snare (Luke 21:34)*

3 *Jesus answered them, "Destroy this temple, and in three days I will raise it up." The Jews then said, "It has taken forty-six years to build this temple" (John 2:19–20)*

❶ The fig tree is one of the most common trees in Palestine. The ideal of safety in peace was for every man to dwell "under his vine and under his fig tree" (I Kings 4:25). This was true not only of the days of Solomon, but also during the times of the prophets (Mic. 4:4), and of the Achaemenids (Zech. 3:10). Quite often, vines and fig trees existed in the same enclosure (Luke 13:6) and sometimes the vine clung to the branches of the tree. The fig tree was a harbinger, for its buds appeared very early, shortly after the end of winter. In this respect, the text might be confusing to a Westerner since, according to Jesus, this budding

would announce not the approach of spring, but the approach of summer. The explanation is that for the Palestinian, from time immemorial, the year has had only two seasons instead of four: winter and summer. This is indicated even during the time of Genesis (8:22). That is the whole story.

❷ This image seems to us to come from an old oriental belief. The Old Testament utilizes the image, for instance, in Habakkuk 1:15, Isaiah 24:17, Hosea 7:12, and Ezekiel 32:3. This snare is of the type used to capture birds. Its origin goes back beyond the Old Testament world to Sumer. On the Stele of the Vultures (discovered at Telloh, and dating from the first half of the 3rd millennium B.C.), we see the god Ningirsuk in the process of bludgeoning the enemies of Lagash, who are enclosed in a net. King Eannatum elsewhere boasts of having thrown the net of Enlil, another great deity of the country, over the king's enemies.

❸ When these words were spoken, the temple had not yet been finished; indeed, much remained to be done on it. The statement undoubtedly means that they had

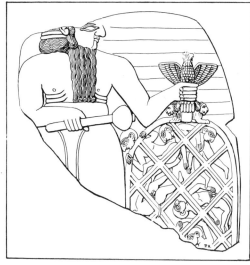

94. Stele of the Vultures. The net of Ningirsuk.

1 *And as Moses lifted up the serpent in the wilderness (John 3:14)*
2 *"There are yet four months, then comes the harvest" (John 4:35)*
3 *Now there is in Jerusalem by the Sheep Gate a pool, in Hebrew called Bethzatha, which has five porticoes (John 5:2)*

been working on it for forty-six years. This information provides an excellent chronological base for Jesus' ministry. According to Josephus, Herod had the work started in the eighteenth year of his reign (elsewhere, he says the fifteenth), or in 20–19 B.C. Forty-six years later would put us at A.D. 27–28.

❶ This is an allusion to Numbers 21:9. According to this account, Moses made a bronze serpent and set it on a pole. Anyone bitten by a serpent could look at the bronze serpent and live. This is a frequently mentioned feature in oriental antiquity: the image of an injurious being is a means not only of protecting oneself from it but of transforming a maleficent power into a beneficent one. In the land of Sumer, at the end of the 3rd millennium B.C., the serpent became a sacred emblem and was carried processionally. Two intertwined serpents (the prototype of our caduceus) had a salutary quality. Such an emblem was engraved on the libation cup of Prince Gudea. This same belief is attested in the Canaanite city of Hazor, where there is a bronze plaque decorated with a deity who holds two serpents in his hands. This plaque was affixed to the end of a staff, as if indicating that it was an appendage which extended the staff.

95.   The Sheep Gate at Jerusalem.

❷ These four months undoubtedly are those which separate the sowing from the harvesting. For barley, the harvest could begin around April 15, and for wheat, in June. The month of May would be the month when one could say that the fields were white for harvest. The four months were mentioned as early as the 9th century B.C. on the agricultural calendar of Gezer. They come up again in a text from Qumran.

❸ The Sheep Gate received its name from the fact that through it sheep destined for sacrifice in the temple were brought into the city. It was located in the north wall, between the Tower of Hananel and the northeast corner of the fortification. Evidently it was at the site of what is now Herod's Gate, where forty years ago there was still a sheep market. The name of the pool is not certain, for the manuscripts give several variant readings: Bethsaida, Bethesda ("house of mercy"), Belzetha, Bethzatha, Bezatha, Bezetha.

An installation has been discovered on the property of the White Fathers near St. Anne's Church which almost certainly can be identified with the pool of the Gospel. Excavations were begun in 1871 and pursued sporadically until finally in 1956 they were begun again in a systematic fashion. They are still being conducted. Although they will probably necessitate a modification of the plan which Father Vincent has proposed recently, the excavations confirm the veneration of the site as the place where the miracle took place, a veneration which existed during the Byzantine era and which was continued by the Crusaders. The numerous votive offerings which have been discovered at the site indicate that during Jesus' time there was a pool there placed under the invocation of Serapis and Asclepius, two healing gods. One of these votive offerings is in the Louvre: the foot of Pompeia Lucilia. This offering indicates that a

96. Foot of Pompeia Lucilia. *Museum of the Louvre.*

healing had taken place; it was offered by the former sick person to the deity whose presence had conferred miraculous properties on the spring.[1] The therapeutic and

[1] Cf. *Le Musée du Louvre et la Bible*, pp. 145–46.

100

1 *After this Jesus went to the other side of the Sea of Galilee, which is the Sea of Tiberias (John 6:1)*

2 *Now the Jews' feast of Tabernacles was at hand (John 7:2)*

radioactive qualities of certain waters need no longer be demonstrated, but the ancients would never have supposed anything but that a deity activated such waters. By healing the paralytic at the pool of Bethzatha, Jesus gave the demonstration of his power, which was manifested simply by the words: "Rise, take up your pallet, and walk." At the same time, he achieved a victory over the gods of classical paganism which had been introduced into the very heart of Jerusalem, the city of Yahweh.

❶ According to the Evangelist, Jesus is once again in Galilee. It has been observed that John gives a version of Jesus' activity which differs greatly from that found in the Synoptics. Jesus, in the Gospel of John, moves about continuously: Galilee (miracle at Cana), Jerusalem (the merchants in the temple, the encounter with Nicodemus), Samaria (Jacob's well), Galilee (healing of the official's son), Jerusalem (miracle at the pool of Bethzatha), once again in Galilee. John is also the only one to mention Tiberias, the city founded by Herod Antipas and at its height during Jesus' day. One may believe that John took a certain pleasure in mentioning the city (6:23; 21:1), even though Jesus himself had not had any ministry there. In any case, Tiberias was to

remain for many centuries the metropolis of rabbinical Judaism. In the 2nd century A.D., the Sanhedrin was transferred there, with the school from which came the Mishnah (collection of Jewish traditions), the Gemara (supplement to these traditions), and, finally, the Massorah. The latter is concerned with the fixing of the pronunciation and punctuation of the Old Testament text. Up until that time, the text was composed solely of consonants, and the Massoretes provided a system of vowel points. At Tiberias the celebrated rabbis Akiba (2nd century A.D.) and Maimonides (A.D. 1135–1204) are supposed to have been buried. Christianity took root there only at the time of Constantine. Today, like all of Galilee, Tiberias is in Israeli territory.

❷ The Feast of Tabernacles began on the 15th of Tishri (September–October) and lasted for one week. It commemorated the end of the harvest and, at the same time, the sojourn in the wilderness. On this occasion, the Israelites lived in booths (*sukkoth*) of foliage. In the temple there were processions and libations of water on the altar. It was during the course of one of these celebrations that the high priest, Alexander Janneus (d. 76 B.C.), was bombarded with citrons brought for the feast. This was a

1 *Does he intend to go to the Dispersion among the Greeks and teach the Greeks? (John 7:35)*

2 *Jesus stood up and proclaimed, "If any one thirst, let him come to me and drink. He who believes in me, as the scripture has said, 'Out of his heart shall flow rivers of living water' " (John 7:37–38)*

3 *Jesus bent down and wrote with his finger on the ground (John 8:6,8)*

demonstration of bad humor, if not hostility, on the part of those who were worshiping there. In such a gathering of people, Jesus had a good occasion to let himself be seen. This is what his brothers counseled him to do, and in the end this is what he did (7:10). This, then, was a new visit to Jerusalem, the third one, in John's view.

❶ This passage refers primarily to the colonies of Jews who lived outside of the Holy Land, that is, the Diaspora. There were such colonies in Phoenicia, in Asia Minor, in Egypt, in Greece, and even in Rome. One understood the term "Greeks" to mean "foreigners."

❷ The libations which were offered during the Feast of Tabernacles quite naturally focused attention on water. This is the background of Jesus' intervention. Although the latter is related to the Scriptures, exegetes are agreed in the opinion that we do not know the precise text to which Jesus alludes. Isaiah 58:11, whatever may be said for it, is fairly far removed from Jesus' allusion. What is most striking to us is that the passage, as we have already written,[1] is an extraordinary and impressive reminiscence of Mesopotamian iconography: monuments from the 3rd, 2nd, and 1st millennia often have representations of male or female deities holding waist-high, in both hands, a vase from which water flows. Rivers literally flow from the heart of the personage represented. Two scholars, Rudolph Bultmann and Millar Burrows, have made the same comparison. They do not explain it, nor do we, but it is nonetheless striking.

97. Gushing vases. *Museum of the Louvre.*

❸ This passage comes from the incident of the adulterous woman, which some exegetes would omit from the Gospel of John, although they do not question its authenticity. Those who brought to Jesus the woman who had been caught in the very act hoped thereby to put him into opposition with the Law of Moses. Before replying, Jesus knelt and wrote "on the ground."

[1] *Le Musée du Louvre et la Bible,* p. 13.

1 *These words he spoke in the treasury, as he taught in the temple (John 8:20)*

2 *Go, wash in the pool of Siloam (John 9:7)*

3 *The Good Shepherd (John 10)*

4 *The good shepherd lays down his life for the sheep (John 10:11)*

It has often been wondered what he wrote. At first glance, this behavior might appear rather odd. On this point again we are reminded of the children among our workers, who very often amuse themselves by writing in the sand or in the very fine dirt of our excavations. Every time we see them do this, we cannot help making the comparison with the Johannine episode.

98. The "Good Shepherd."

❶ The treasury (*gazophulakion*) was located in the Court of the Women, thus beyond the enclosure which the Gentiles could not pass.

❷ This reservoir was located to the south of Jerusalem, within the wall. It was fed by an underground canal which had been constructed on the orders of Hezekiah (716–687 B.C.). The canal carried water from the Virgin's Spring (Gihon in the Old Testament; today called Um ed-Daradj, "the mother of degrees"). In the 5th century, a church was built above the pool to commemorate the healing. Very little remains of the church. Moreover, the whole region during the past ten years has undergone so many transformations and constructions that it has become unrecognizable to anyone acquainted with it thirty years ago. A small mosque has replaced the Byzantine church.

❸ In a country like Palestine, and especially in Judea, Jesus found examples in the life of the flocks, examples which all would have before their eyes and from which he could draw a lesson.

❹ At the beginning of the monarchy, David could remind Saul that sometimes he had had to save sheep of his father's flocks from the mouths of lions or bears (I Sam.

1 *All who came before me are thieves and robbers (John 10:8)*

2 *It was the feast of the Dedication at Jerusalem; it was winter, and Jesus was walking in the temple, in the portico of Solomon (John 10:22–23)*

3 *The resurrection of Lazarus (John 11:1–46)*

17:34–35). Sometimes the shepherd was less lucky, and could bring back only "two legs, or a piece of an ear" (Amos 3:12), which is an indication of the ravages committed by wild beasts (Gen. 31:39; Exod. 22:13).

Shepherding was not all rest and repose for the shepherd, and Jesus, knowing the dangers of the job, pointed out the difference in behavior between the person who owns his own flock and the person who is hired to watch over someone else's flock.

❶ In speaking thus, Jesus certainly is not thinking of Moses or the Prophets, the heroes of the Old Covenant, nor of John the Baptist, who had been executed at the prison of Machaerus. Quite probably he is thinking of the false messiahs who often appeared in the Jewish world. One example, perhaps, would be Judas the Galilean, during the time of the census of Quirinius in A.D. 6 (Acts 5:37). Theudas, who also is mentioned in Acts (5:36), appeared later, around A.D. 44, and thus after Jesus had spoken these words. Both Judas the Galilean and Theudas were simply adventurers.

❷ This feast lasted eight days, beginning on Chislev 25 (in December) and lasting until Tebet 2 (in January). It commemorated the purification of the temple of Jerusalem, which had been profaned by Antiochus Epiphanes. On Chislev 25 of the year 165 B.C., Judas Maccabeus purified the temple (I Macc. 4:36–59; II Macc. 1:9, 18; 10:1–8). This feast is still celebrated by the Jews under the name of Hanukkah. It is also called the Festival of Lights, an appelation which has been given to it since the time of Josephus. Just as in some Christian homes one candle is lit on each of the Sundays of Advent (which gives a total of four, the last being lit on the Sunday before Christmas), so in contemporary Judaism the lights are increased by one each night of the festival (one candle on the first night, eight on the last). Since it was wintertime, the humid and cold season, it was normal that those who were in the temple would remain under the porticoes. Solomon's Portico was on the east side, overlooking the Kidron.

❸ The account in John fits in directly with that in Luke (10:38–39). Luke gives the names of Martha and Mary, but does not give the name of the village where they lived, nor the name of their brother Lazarus. Jesus learned of Lazarus' sickness in Perea (John 10:40; 11:6), thus on the other side of the Jordan. *Lazarus*, a variant form of the name Eleazar ("God has helped"), was a common name in New Testament times.

99. Ossuary.

Bethany, or "House of Ananiah" (cf. Neh. 11:32), is the modern el-Azariyeh; it was located on the eastern slope of the Mount of Olives, beyond Bethphage. The name "Martha" is Aramaic ("lady"); "Mary" is the Greek form of the Hebrew "Myriam." All of these names — Martha, Eleazar, Mary — have been found in ossuary inscriptions.

This obviously does not mean that the Gospel personages are the ones referred to, but simply that these names were present in New Testament times.

By the time Jesus arrived at Bethany, Lazarus had been dead four days. Martha learned that Jesus was coming and went to meet him. She thus went east, beyond the village.

1 *Now among those who went up to worship at the feast were some Greeks. So these came to Philip, who was from Bethsaida in Galilee, and said to him, "Sir, we wish to see Jesus" (John 12:20–21)*

2 *Maundy Thursday to Easter Sunday*

This is the reason — and the only reason — why the Greek Orthodox have built a church at Deir el-Jenaineh, to the east of el-Azariyeh. After speaking first with Martha, and then with Mary, who had also hastened to meet him, Jesus went to the tomb. The term employed to characterize the tomb (*spelaion*) indicates that it was a vertical shaft tomb; the opening was closed by means of a stone placed over it. When the stone was removed, Jesus performed a new miracle. Lazarus, still wrapped in the linen strips that had been dipped in aromatics at the time of burial and with his face wrapped in a cloth, came out of the tomb. This tomb has been venerated since the 4th century, but there is no way of affirming that the site which guides point out today was the actual location of the tomb. Even if it is authentic, it has under-gone so many alterations that its original appearance has long since disappeared.

❶ These "Greeks" were originally from Greco-Roman paganism. They had become Jewish proselytes after an energetic propaganda effort on the part of the Jews of the Diaspora. They were called "god-fearers" (cf. Acts 10:2; 13:16), but also "proselytes of the gate" (because they were not integrated into the Jewish community). Strictly speaking, Bethsaida was not in Galilee, since the territory beyond the Jordan did not belong to Herod Antipas but to the tetrarch Philip. The close proximity of the Decapolis suggests that this whole area was quite hellenized. The names Philip and Andrew were Greek names; perhaps this explains why the Greeks at Jerusalem addressed themselves first to Philip and why he then went to consult Andrew.

VII. Maundy Thursday to Easter Sunday

❷ The last two days of Jesus' life are not recounted by the Synoptics in the same way that they are by the Fourth Gospel. In Matthew, Mark, and Luke, Jesus and his disciples ate on Thursday evening a meal which resembled in certain respects the Passover meal (Mark 14:12; Matt. 26:17; Luke 22:7). It was during the course of this meal that the Lord's Supper was instituted. According to John, on the contrary, the Last Supper was not a Passover meal. It is said quite explicitly that when Jesus appeared before Pilate, the Jews had not yet eaten the Passover (John 18:28). On the other hand, the institution of the Lord's Supper is not reported; rather, John reports the episode of the foot-washing (13:3–11), which is reported nowhere else. These divergences are considerable and nothing is to be gained by minimizing them. We shall see if it is possible to reconcile these differences and, if so, how.

Although the feast of the Passover existed *before* the Exodus from Egypt, it had become among the Jews primarily a commemoration of the Exodus (Exod. 12:6–11), thus the commemoration of deliverance. The lamb, which had been set apart for four days, was sacrificed on Nisan 14 and eaten on the following evening, that is, on Nisan 15 (Nisan corresponds to our month of March–April). The pascal meal was composed of the roasted flesh of the lamb, bitter herbs, unleavened bread cut into four pieces, all of which was inserted into a succession of prayers, readings, and the singing of psalms. From the beginning of Nisan 15, for a week only unleavened bread (*azymes*) was eaten in the homes.

Although the Gospels differ in regard to the type of the Last Supper, they are in agreement as far as the day of Jesus' death is concerned: it was a Friday, the day before the sabbath (Mark 15:42; Matt. 27:62; Luke 23:54; John 19:42). The Gospel accounts fix the Last Supper on the evening before, thus on Thursday evening. It was between the beginning of Thursday night and 9 A.M. Friday that all of the important events took place: the meal (paschal or not), with the institution of the Lord's Supper, the episode in Gethsemane, the arrest, appearance before the Sanhedrin, appearance before Pilate, condemnation, and crucifixion (Mark 15:25). We shall see that such a concentration of events was not impossible, and that the obvious haste is easily explained.

A few years ago, following the discovery of the Dead Sea Scrolls, Miss A. Jaubert proposed an alternative unfolding of the events. That year there had been two Passovers: that of official Judaism, of the temple of Jerusalem, which began on Friday evening (Nisan 15, going from sundown on Friday to sundown on Saturday); and that of the dissident priestly circles, including Qumran, which celebrated a Passover three days earlier. According to Miss Jaubert, Jesus had followed the latter tradition. Thus he had not eaten the Passover on *Thursday* evening, as had always been thought, but on *Tuesday* evening (this same thing had been said in the Didache, a Christian work of the 3rd century, and repeated by Epiphanius in the 5th century). Consequently, everything must naturally be shifted: the arrest on Tuesday night, the appearance before the Sanhedrin on Wednesday and Thursday; appearance before Pilate on Thursday and Friday; the crucifixion on Friday. This theory gets rid of the differences: the Tuesday meal was indeed a paschal meal (agreeing with the Synoptics) and the official Passover took place on Friday evening (with John).

The theory is attractive, but it is not without its faults. The principal criticism of it is that it is based on a postulate that has not yet been proven: the influence of Essenism on Jesus' actions. Jesus would have had to break off from official Judaism in order to follow a dissident calendar — and this, on such an important point as the celebration of the Passover. Also, to fix the Last Supper on Tuesday is to go against the whole Gospel tradition, which places it on Thursday. To place the institution of the Lord's Supper at some other time would be to go against the testimony of Saint Paul, who is our earliest witness regarding the time of the event: "on the night that he was betrayed" (I Cor. 11:23). To say that Jesus had not eaten the Passover with his disciples on Maundy Thursday would be to refuse to recognize that even though the accounts of the evening make no explicit reference to it, the lamb is implicitly the concern of the accounts. For what would be the meaning of "prepare . . . to eat the Passover" (Mark 14:12, 16; Matthew 26:17–19; Luke 22:8–9, 13), except to kill the animal, make the unleavened bread, prepare the bitter herbs and the ritual beverage? On the other hand, there remain the precise details of the Johannine chronology: the Passover could not begin before Friday evening. These details are as categorical as those of the Synoptics.

The accounts appear to be contradictory and therefore irreconcilable. Is it sufficient to say, with Father Benoit, that the Synoptics have given a "fully paschal character to what in reality could only have been an anticipated evocation of the Passover of the following day, with the institution of a new rite which was destined to replace the Passover"? Should one go further and think, with Father Lagrange, that "it does not seem to be impossible that a given group had celebrated the Passover on the day be-

1 *Then the chief priests and the elders of the people . . . took counsel together in order to arrest Jesus by stealth and kill him (Matthew 26:3–4)*

2 *Then one of the twelve, who was called Judas Iscariot, went to the chief priests and said, "What will you give me if I deliver him to you?" And they paid him thirty pieces of silver (Matthew 26:14–15)*

3 *The first day of Unleavened Bread (Matthew 26:17; Mark 14:12; Luke 22:7)*

4 *Go into the city, and a man carrying a jar of water will meet you (Mark 14:13–14; Luke 22:10–11)*

fore the official day"? And that this group would be the Galileans, who enjoyed certain tolerated privileges? Such hypotheses are based on no textual evidence, but still they are maintained, for they seem worthy of belief. Two points remain, which we feel are solidly established: Jesus had spent the Passover with his disciples on Thursday evening, but the official Passover had not been celebrated until the following day, Friday evening.[1] What was the reason for this earlier celebration? This is what scholars have not yet been able to explain in any acceptable way. Perhaps it is best to let it go at that, for it changes nothing in the fact of the matter.

❶ Those involved in this conspiracy constituted a part of the Sanhedrin, which at the time of Jesus was composed of the priests (sacrificers) and elders (laity). All that are lacking in this passage are the scribes, who are mentioned elsewhere (Mark 14:1; Luke 22:1). The presidency was always in the hands of the high priest, who in Jesus' day was Caiaphas.

[1] A chronological summary of the Passion following both traditions, the Synoptic and the Johannine, is given in Table III.

❷ The price of the betrayal is evaluated in shekels, which was the basic unit of weighing precious metals. The shekel weighed 16.37 grams and was worth about sixty-five cents.

❸ According to our calculation, this "first day of Unleavened Bread" was Nisan 13 (from sundown Wednesday to sundown Thursday), Nisan 14 beginning at sundown Thursday. Nisan 14 was the day on which one "prepared the Passover," but the lamb had to be sacrificed "between the two nights," that is to say, according to the official date, on Friday morning. Athough we cannot explain it, Jesus had eaten the Passover twenty-four hours before. The preparations were made for his disciples and him before nightfall on Thursday. As the name indicates, the bread contained no leaven. This bread undoubtedly was similar to the cakes so well known in the Orient and the only type currently used among Arab Bedouins and peasants. They are very thin, somewhat crusty slabs of dough baked on ovens.

❹ In Matthew's version (26:18), Jesus gives the name of the owner of the house. Mark and Luke both have the more picturesque detail of the man carrying a jar of water. Such a man would be easy to pick

1 *And he will show you a large upper room furnished and ready (Mark 14:15; Luke 22:12)*

2 *When it was evening, he sat at table with the twelve disciples (Matthew 26:20; Mark 14:17–18; Luke 22:14)*

100. The Upper Room and David's Tomb.

out, since generally it is only the women who go to draw water for the household needs. Whence is he coming? Undoubtedly, from one of the two sources of water in Jerusalem at that time: the spring of Gihon or the pool of Siloam. From there, the man had to mount a steep incline toward the city.

❶ The room offered to the disciples was on the second floor and was the reception room of the house. As in Arab houses of today (we are speaking primarily of the villages), there is no furniture. On the ground, however, are matting and carpets of the *kelim* type. In niches in the walls there are abundant cushions stacked up on

top of one another. When guests arrive, these cushions are brought out and placed at the foot of the walls, to serve as backrests or armrests. Besides being used to receive guests, they are also used at night.

Where was the room of the Last Supper located? Tradition early sought to locate the site beyond the Tyropoeon Valley, on the west slope, at a place today called the Coenaculum. The site of the Last Supper, the institution of the Lord's Supper, the Upper Room of the apostles, the memory of Pentecost: all were concentrated in the same area and consecrated by the erection of a small church. Later a basilica was erected on the site (finished in the 5th century), bearing the name Sainte-Sion. The basilica was completely destroyed, and now the site is occupied by a small mosque and a so-called Tomb of David.

❷ We should not picture in our minds a scene like that represented in the painting by Leonardo da Vinci which adorns the refectory wall in the old Dominican monastery at Milan. If there was a "table" at all, it was a very low one, on which the elements constituting the Passover meal had been placed. As for us, however, we would rather imagine the scene in a specifically Eastern framework: a large brass tray in the

1 *He who has dipped his hand in the dish with me, will betray me (Matthew 26:23; Mark 14:20; Luke 22:21)*

2 *Jesus took bread, and blessed, and broke it (Matthew 26:26; Mark 14:22; Luke 22:19)*

3 *And he took a cup, and when he had given thanks he gave it to them (Matthew 26:27; Mark 14:23; Luke 22:20)*

101.   Chalice of Antioch.

❶ This detail, to be taken literally, confirms what we have just said about there being only one tray with all seated in a circle about it. Since they had no plates, the guests helped themselves, with the right hand, to the food that was on the common platter. A piece of bread, rolled up, served as both fork and plate.

❷ The bread was not cut, but was either broken (if it was well done) or torn (if the baking had been moderate). In any case, a knife was *never* used.

❸ Had there been one cup or several cups at this meal? The question has been much debated, and opinions differ. In an ordinary meal, there is usually only the common cup. But according to the scholars, the Passover ritual involved each person's having his own cup. However, in this meal — which was also the institution of the Lord's Supper — why could not Jesus have taken one cup and then circulated it? One wonders of what material the cup was made. Excavations have yielded up earthenware, metal, and glass cups. Earthenware was the most common, glass the most fragile. We think the cup used at the Last Supper was likely made of metal (here again we take into account contemporary practices).

middle of the room, with the roast lamb in the center. All around the animal, the unleavened bread, the bitter herbs, and a cup. Jesus was seated cross-legged, and, in a circle around the tray, the disciples were seated in a similar manner.

1 *Jesus took bread, and blessed, and broke it, and gave it to the disciples. . . . And he took a cup, and when he had given thanks he gave it to them (Matthew 26:26–27; Mark 14:22–23; Luke 22:19–20)*

A few years ago, a loud noise was made concerning a silver chalice, set in a storied mounting and called the "chalice of Antioch." It was in the hands of antiquarians, the brothers Kouchakji, who indicated this point of origin. Eisen, in 1916, had first called attention to it. In 1931 it was exhibited at Paris and aroused even greater interest, if not sensation, because Eisen asserted that the interior cup was that of Maundy Thursday. It had been miraculously protected, had been carried from Jerusalem to Antioch, and had become a relic of exceptional nature for the primitive church, to judge by its external decor: Christ is represented two times and is surrounded by ten persons, the identifications of whom brought forth different opinions. Either they were the eight writers of the New Testament, plus two of their brothers; or, Christ and the ten disciples present on the evening of the Resurrection (John 20:19–25); or again, the leaders of the churches of Jerusalem and of Antioch. All that in a decor of vine-branches and various emblems (lamb, doves, eagle, crow, etc.), obviously evoking memories from the Gospels. Presently scholars are of the opinion that although the inner cup may be older, the ornamentation surrounding it dates from the 3rd or 4th century. It is certainly one of the oldest chalices of Christian antiquity and, for this reason, a venerable piece of evidence. As for saying that it is the cup of Maundy Thursday, that is a step which we do not believe we can or should take.

The chalice was acquired in 1950 by the Metropolitan Museum. It is not the only one of its kind. It is an example of a well-attested sacred goldsmith trade (Emesa, Riha, Stuma) which gives evidence of the wealth of the Christian churches in that region, infinitely more prosperous than the churches in Palestine.

❶ Theologians and exegetes have long debated the question of whether or not Jesus ate any of the bread he had just broken or drank any of the wine which he had just poured. If the Lord's Supper was a simple meal, and one similar to those of today, the answer would have to be no. In the Orient, the master of the house never touches the meal which he offers you, at least not at the same time as his guests. Abraham, hosting the three strangers (Gen. 18:1–8), stood apart and did not participate in the feast which he had prepared for them. But here, Jesus is "at table" with his disciples. It seems difficult to allow that he

112

1 *Until that day when I drink it new with you in my Father's kingdom (Matthew 26:29; Mark 14:25; Luke 22:18)*

2 *The washing of the disciples' feet (John 13:3–12)*

3 *And when they had sung a hymn, they went out to the Mount of Olives (Matthew 26:30; Mark 14:26)*

did not eat. Indeed, it says explicitly that he did eat — but we can never know whether or not he ate of the bread that he had broken or drank of the wine that he had poured.

❶ Ancient beliefs postulated meals in the world to come. The idea of the feast in the kingdom of God had often been evoked by Jesus (Matt. 8:11; Luke 13:29). Phoenician, Greek, and Aramaean funerary steles show the deceased seated before a table, eating and drinking. The "being seated at table in the kingdom of God" indicates quite well that this idea of posthumous existence was firmly anchored in the Jewish mentality. Jesus refers to it in this image.

❷ As we have said previously, the Fourth Gospel speaks neither of the Passover meal nor of the institution of the Lord's Supper, but of another episode which is not mentioned elsewhere: Jesus washes the feet of his disciples on the last night of his terrestrial life. When the master of the house receives a guest, it is often the custom to welcome him by pouring water on his feet in order to clean off the dust of the road. We must remember that they walked barefoot

or simply in sandals. This custom is attested elsewhere in the Gospels (Luke 7:44), and even in the Old Testament (Gen. 18:4; I Sam. 25:41). No doubt this was a hygienic measure, but it was also a gesture of extreme humility for the one who did it. The same custom is found among the Greeks: on an Attic vase (4th century B.C.) found in Etruria, we see the servant Eurykleia washing over a large bowl the feet of Ulysses on his return to his house.[1]

❸ The exegetes who consider the meal to have been a "paschal" one take into account the fact that psalms were sung, which was a part of the Jewish ritual of the feast. Jesus and his disciples left the Upper Room and headed toward the city, in the direction of the Mount of Olives. One would love to know their route. It is not impossible that in order to go down to the city, the group took a long path of stairs which have been rediscovered on the slope of the Gallicante and which could have existed in Jesus' day.

[1] Reproduced in *Views of the Biblical World*, 5, *The New Testament*, p. 149.

1 *He went forth with his disciples across the Kidron valley, where there was a garden, which he and his disciples entered (John 18:1)*

❶ The group first had to go up the Kidron Valley on the right bank, then cross it just after having passed in front of the tombs cut into the rocks (Jehoshaphat, Absalom, Saint James, Zechariah). They came immediately to a garden whose name has been recorded by Matthew (26:36) and Mark (14:32): Gethsemane, which lies at the foot of the Mount of Olives. The four Evangelists (see also Luke 22:39) are quite definite regarding the site: a garden on the other side of the stream, at the Mount of Olives. This could not have been higher than the Gethsemane of today, due to the slope which rapidly becomes steeper and which does not provide a good stopping place. The area was planted with olive trees, and still is. The name "Gethsemane" means "oil press."

102. "Stairway of Maundy Thursday."
103. Gethsemane and the Mount of Olives.

1 *Now the betrayer had given them a sign, saying, "The one I shall kiss is the man" (Matthew 26:48; Mark 14:44; Luke 22:47)*

2 *And a young man followed him, with nothing but a linen cloth about his body; and they seized him, but he left the linen cloth and ran away naked (Mark 14:51–52)*

❶ Judas' kiss is not an extraordinary thing, or an unusual gesture. In the Orient, it is a sign of respect and of veneration to take the hand of a great personage while at the same time kissing him on the shoulder. Judas quite probably took a similar attitude. In this particular case, it was also the sign of treason.

❷ This is a curious episode which only Mark reports. It is certainly authentic. One has the impression that it was a matter of someone nearby who had been awakened from his sleep and who ran to see what all the noise was about (for a large troop coming to make an arrest also makes a lot of noise).

The person was not dressed. He wore only the light robe in which he had wrapped himself for sleep, and which he now draped about him. Since they were going to arrest him also, he struggled and, leaving behind his improvised clothing, ran away as fast as possible, with nothing on his back. Some scholars have thought that the person concerned here was the Evangelist Mark, who would have wanted to recall this minor incident in which he was, despite himself, the hero; this would have permitted him to provide an eyewitness account of the arrest. Such an identification is not self-evident. It would need to be explained why Mark was in the area in clothing not really adequate

104. The Garden of Gethsemane.

1 *While he was still speaking, Judas came, one of the twelve, and with him a great crowd with swords and clubs (Matthew 26:47; Mark 14:43)*

2 *Then those who had seized Jesus led him to Caiaphas the high priest, where the scribes and the elders had gathered (Matthew 26:57; Mark 14:53; Luke 22:54)*

for a nocturnal sortie, unless, obviously, he came from a house nearby. But no tradition has recorded that Mark owned a house at Gethsemane or in the immediate vicinity.

❶ This detail has an astonishing realism about it. Those who have seen anything of riot or uprising in the Orient will not be surprised at such a varied armament. During the time of the British mandate in Palestine (that is, between 1920 and 1948), the Palestinian police were often equipped with staunch cudgels as well as bayonets. This was the case, for example, on the day of rioting at the Holy Sepulcher. Regular soldiers (John 18:3 mentions the cohort) could indeed have been provided with these disparate weapons: swords and clubs. However, let us leave these weapons in the hands of the troop which Judas guided. Since Jesus had lately become accustomed to spending the nights on the Mount of Olives (Luke 22:39), the traitor did not have to seek far; he had accompanied the Master on the preceding evenings (John 18:2).

❷ According to tradition, the house of Caiaphas was near the Coenaculum, on the site presently occupied by the Armenian Convent of the Holy Savior. Since the

Byzantine period there have been first a church and then a medieval chapel (a short distance away) at the site. At Caiaphas' house there was a meeting of the scribes, the elders, and the chief priests (or sacrificers), that is to say, the members of the Sanhedrin.

105. An olive tree in Gethsemane.

116

1 *And Peter had followed him at a distance, right into the courtyard of the high priest; and he was sitting with the guards, and warming himself at the fire (Mark 14:54; Matthew 26:58; Luke 22:54–55)*

106. "The house of Caiaphas."

❶ The Fourth Gospel adds a new detail: Peter was not alone, but had followed "with another disciple." This disciple is not named. He was known to the high priest, and even better to the high priest's personnel, and was thus able to gain Peter's entrance into the interior. Indeed, one would presuppose that a check was made at the door and that not just anybody could enter.

The whole scene is extraordinarily lifelike: the house of the high priest was built on the

inner court plan, open to the sky, with the rooms of the building opening on the court. Since winter was just past, it was very cold during the late hours of the night. A fire was burning in the courtyard and everybody was seated around it, trying to keep warm. Jesus had been led into the reception hall, which must have been located on the second floor (thus we could better understand Mark 14:66, which says that "Peter was below"). From there, Jesus could look down on the court and on all that was happening there, since the rooms on the upper levels also opened onto the court. Thus, when Peter had denied him for the third time, the Lord, by turning around, could regard his disciple (Luke 22:61). At this instant, a cock crowed. Peter, recalling Jesus' words, left and wept bitterly.

During the Middle Ages there was a church consecrated to this incident, named Saint-Pierre au Gallicante ("Saint Peter's of the crowing of the cock"). In the enclosure of the Assumptionist Fathers, lower than the Armenian Convent of the Holy Savior, a modern church has been built in commemoration of this moment. But it cannot claim to have preserved the site of the house of Caiaphas.

117

We have seen previously that John mentions the cohort (that is, an armed Roman force) at the time of the arrest in Gethsemane; he also affirms its presence at the house of Caiaphas. Beforehand the same Evangelist (and, once again, he alone) mentions that Jesus had first been led to Annas (John 18:13), but we know that Annas had lost his office at the hands of the procurator Valerius Gratus. He undoubtedly had retained a great authority, but he could not preside over the Sanhedrin, which was the exclusive prerogative of the high priest then in office. This, of course, was Caiaphas, to whom the prisoner was then sent (John 18:24).

Jesus appeared before the Sanhedrin. Had the complete number of seventy-one members been convoked? We do not know. Normally, the Sanhedrin sat in a special hall, east of the Xystus, a porticoed gymnasium built by Herod the Great between the temple and the Palace of the Hasmoneans. This time, however, the Sanhedrin met in the house of the high priest. The authority of the Sanhedrin of Jerusalem varied according to the continually changing political regimes. It seems that during the time of Jesus the Sanhedrin's jurisdiction extended over all of the Jews in the Empire, but its coercive power existed only in Judea. It could hear all types of cases, but, from the time of the annexation of Judea as a Roman province, the death sentence could be carried out only after the approval of the procurator. Jesus, judged deserving of death for blasphemy (he had declared himself "Son of God"), thus had to be taken to Pilate. But since the interrogation took place at night (the second crowing of the cock, in Mark 14:72, indicates that it was about 5 A.M.), the decision risked being nullified; thus a second meeting took place (Matt. 27:1; Mark 15:1; Luke 22:66), this time during the day. It is not impossible that more members attended this second meeting, since more time was available to call them all together. Distances are not great in Jerusalem, and comings and goings are easy and rapid. The second assembly had only to ratify what had been decided an hour earlier.

❶ Just before the convergence of the three valleys which border or traverse Jerusalem (Kidron, Tyropoeon, and Ge-Hinnom, i.e., Gehenna), at the cut of the Ge-Hinnom, one may see a half-ruined edifice which served as a common tomb for "strangers" (Matt. 27:7), that is, pilgrims who had died at Jerusalem. Here tradition

1 *And they bound Jesus and led him away and delivered him to Pilate (Mark 15:1; Matthew 27:2; Luke 23:1)*

locates the suicide of Judas. However, there are two versions. According to Matthew, the priests took the thirty pieces of silver, which Judas had returned before doing away with himself, and bought the field with the money. The second version, Acts 1:18–19) says that the traitor had bought the field with the reward of his wickedness and that it was only later that he killed himself. It was called "the potter's field," evidently because there was a pottery workshop there, a factory for those "earthen vessels" (Isa. 45:9; II Cor. 4:7) which excavations in the Orient have unearthed by the thousands.

❶ Pontius Pilate was procurator of Judea from A.D. 26 to 36. The fifth Roman governor since the deposition of Archelaus (A.D. 6), he came to Palestine, with his wife, to replace Valerius Gratus. He was eventually recalled to Rome to answer for the severe repression of the Samaritans, who, at the call of a visionary, had undertaken excavations on Mount Gerizim in search of a golden plate which was supposed to have been hidden there by Moses.

Up to recent times, all that we have known of Pilate was provided by the Gospels and by the Jewish historian Josephus. In 1961, however, Italian archaeologists discovered a

107. Akeldama.

block at Caesarea (the block had been re-employed in the construction of an ancient theater) inscribed with four lines mentioning specifically Tiberius and Pilate. This is the first archaeological testimony to the procurator. It is not surprising that it was discovered at Caesarea, since this was the customary residence of the Roman official.

119

However, he came to Jerusalem for the great Jewish festivals. These occasions could bring trouble, and consequently needed constant surveillance. Thus, quite naturally, Pilate was at Jerusalem for this particular Passover.

Where was his residence (or "tribunal" or "praetorium")? There are two contrary theses. According to the first (Father Vincent), Pilate resided at the Antonia, that is, in the fortress which Herod the Great had built at the northwest corner of the temple. The sisters of Notre-Dame de Sion believe the Basilica of the Ecce Homo to be located on the precise spot where the procurator handed over to the Jews for crucifixion "the Man" whom they had brought before his tribunal. A magnificent section of pavement reappeared under the sanctuary, extending over some 2100 square yards; it goes back at the latest to Herod Agrippa II (d. A.D. 100). Some of these slabs are engraved with symbols undoubtedly related to games. One can easily imagine the soldiers of the temple guard occupying their leisure time playing chess or throwing dice on these awkwardly drawn squares.

According to the second thesis (Father Abel, Dalman, J. Jeremias, and, recently, Father Benoit), it was obligatory that, during his visits to Jerusalem, the Judean procurator reside at the old Palace of Herod the Great, which today is the site of the Tower of David (not far from the Jaffa Gate). The tribune was at the Antonia, the procurator at the palace. Thus the city was watched over quite well. The praetorium, therefore, must be located at Pilate's residence in the palace; this seems to be the best solution in our present state of knowledge. As the crow flies, it is about 550 yards from the house of Caiaphas to the residence of Pilate. For a slow-moving procession such as that which led Jesus to Pilate, it would take about fifteen minutes.

It was at the beginning of day, since the second meeting of the Sanhedrin must not have taken very long. Let us say it was about 7 A.M. (cf. John 18:28). In the Orient, life begins again with the rising of the sun. There is a rhythm to it with which we in the West are not acquainted. The day, then, had already begun when the Jews arrived at Pilate's residence.

❶ The appearance before Pilate is related by John with more details than we find in the Synoptics. The essential difference between John and the Synoptics, however, is in regard to the day: he says quite precisely that it is Nisan 14, the day of the preparation of the Passover. That is, it was the day when the lamb would be sacrificed. It would be eaten at night, which would be Nisan 15, since the days began at sundown. This is why the Jews who led Jesus to the governor remained outside the praetorium in order not to be defiled (John 18:28).

What is meant by the "praetorium"? Quite probably it was the residence of the Roman official, which at Jerusalem we locate in the old Palace of Herod. The result of this, according to the Fourth Gospel, was a whole series of comings and goings between the interior where Pilate was and the exterior where the crowd was (John 18:29, 33, 38; 19:4, 9, 13). The governor made the accused enter, in order to interrogate him in his turn. Was all of this part of the rules? Could a Roman trial be superimposed on a Jewish trial? Several scholars have felt that the accounts are based on two traditions: one tradition attributed the initiative in the events to the Jews; the other attributed it to the Romans, which would explain the presence in Gethsemane of the cohort and a tribune, that is, of Roman soldiers and an officer (John 18:12).

It is not our purpose here to enter into a detailed discussion such as would involve (and has involved) legal opinion. Yet it seems, if one reads the texts without preconceived ideas, that certain clear items appear, precisely from the information given by John (who is the only one to mention the Romans and whose witness could not be suspect). The Jews had judged Jesus deserving of death, since according to them he had "blasphemed" (Matt. 26:65–66; Mark 14:64; Luke 22:71). Yet they could carry out a death sentence only with the approval of the procurator. This is what John says with the greatest clarity: "The Jews said to him [Pilate], 'It is not lawful for us to put any man to death'" (John 18:31). But this matter of a routine approval did not bar Pilate from entering into the heart of the matter. This explains why the Jews, when before Pilate's tribunal, were forced to transform what had been a religious trial before their Sanhedrin into a political affair. "Jesus called himself king," said an agitator. "He dissuades people from paying tax to the state." Even in John, alongside the religious question which cannot be dodged (19:7), there is a clear insistence on the political reasons: Jesus called himself king; consequently the Roman power must consider him suspect (19:12).

1 *Jesus before Herod (Luke 23:6–12)*

2 *The condemnation of Jesus (Matthew 27:15–31; Mark 15:6–20; Luke 23:13–25; John 19:1–16)*

❶ Of the Evangelists, Luke alone reports an appearance before Herod. The man in question was the tetrarch Herod Antipas, who had come from Galilee to Jerusalem, also for the Passover. Pilate had learned that Jesus was a Galilean, and was overjoyed to send him to the prince. Nothing came of this interlude, for Herod was not at all ready to compromise himself, nor did he have any authority in the case, since the affair took place at Jerusalem. The incident provided him the opportunity of seeing one of whom he had heard so much and whom he had long desired to meet (Luke 9:9). The scene, if it is authentic, must have taken place in the Palace of the Hasmoneans, located at Jerusalem, between the temple and the Palace of Herod (praetorium). The location was about 450 yards from Herod's Palace. But this incident was only a brief digression, and Jesus was returned to the praetorium. The events then moved precipitously towards their denouement, but not without Pilate's having shown the greatest hesitation. The Gospels, John especially, are explicit on this point.

❷ Pilate and Jesus were once again face to face. The governor was more and more convinced that the political grounds for the complaint were nonexistent. The Synoptics credit him with one final intervention, namely, that of putting an alternative before the accusers: either Jesus or Barabbas, a common criminal, could be freed. The Jews, contrary to his expectation, chose Barabbas. The latter would be freed and Jesus would be crucified. Crucifixion was a Roman punishment, but the Jews practiced it also. The Hasmonean Alexander Janneus had executed six hundred Pharisees in this manner.

Pilate then proceeded to make his solemn decision. Here again, the information comes from John. The procurator, facing the people (thus he is outside the praetorium), had the *bema* brought out (*bema* can signify either a dais or the tribunal). He "sat down" on it, that is to say, since all judgments had to be pronounced while seated, Pilate was following the rule and was seated on his curule chair (*sella curulis*) on the *bema* when he pronounced judgment.

John is alone in having given another detail, which is the name of the place where the *bema* was placed. It was called *Lithostrotos* in Greek, *Gabbatha* in Aramaic. The former term is applied to a mosaic area as well as to a pavement. In this regard, the paved area discovered in the area of the Tower of

1 *Pilate . . . took water and washed his hands before the crowd (Matthew 27:24)*

2 *A purple robe (John 19:2; Matthew 27:28; Mark 15:17)*

3 *A crown of thorns . . . on his head (Matthew 27:29; Mark 15:17; John 19:2)*

Antonia is mentioned as a reason for thinking that the praetorium was located there. But as we have said previously, there is not sufficient justification for concluding that the praetorium was located in the Tower of Antonia. The Aramaic term is not the Semitic equivalent of *lithostrotos*. Its meaning is disputed; it perhaps can mean "plateau," but also "hill" (which would fit the case of Herod's Palace, located on a ridge). Uncertainty remained up to the last minute. Finally Pilate yielded: Jesus was lost.

❶ Pilate's gesture has become proverbial, and means something like: "That's none of my business. Do as you want to. I don't have any stake in it, nor is it any longer my responsibility." In the present case, did this gesture have the same meaning? One wonders. Perhaps it had another indication, namely, that this affair was settled and done with, as when the auctioneer bangs his gavel and cries "Sold!" But here, what merchandise! The life of a man, and of an innocent man to boot!

❷ According to the Synoptics, the initiative came from the soldiers, who in this way mocked the man who had called himself "king." One could wonder how Roman soldiers ever managed to procure such a piece of wearing apparel. It certainly was not a part of their government issue. Luke helps us out of this difficulty, for he recounts that Jesus had been sent to Herod Antipas, and says explicitly that the latter, after having mocked Jesus, sent him back arrayed in "gorgeous apparel" (Luke 23: 11). There is every reason to believe that "gorgeous apparel" and "purple cloak" were one and the same. Such a costume would certainly not be lacking in the wardrobe of the tetrarch, that prince who was playing the king.

❸ This is another example of barrack-room joking. Botanists have tried to identify these thorns, which are called *acanthe* in the Greek. Nearly all of the possible species of Palestinian flora have been listed, among which the favored choices are *Acanthus spinosus* or *Paliurus spina-christi*.

But, as was the case with the cloak, can we really imagine that the Roman soldiers would have had one or the other of these species at their disposition? This seems highly improbable. We would propose a much simpler solution. Was not this "crown of thorns" simply a handful of ratab, that is, those bushy, skeletal, and thorny bushes

1 *A reed in his right hand (Matthew 27:29)*

2 *Pilate . . . having scourged Jesus, delivered him to be crucified (Matthew 27:26; Mark 15:15; Luke 23:22; John 19:1)*

which grow throughout the Orient and which the women carry home on their backs to be used as fuel? Each house has its provision of ratab, and since it was the winter season the praetorium of Pilate must have had its provision. A soldier needed only to reach out and grab a clump of it. A few branches broken, then braided, and one has a crown. *The* crown. . . .

❶ Only Matthew has mentioned this last piece of mocking: a reed simulating a scepter. Mark also speaks of a reed, but puts it in the hands of the soldiers who use it to strike Jesus (Mark 15:19; cf. also Matt. 27:30). The other two Evangelists do not mention a reed at all. Reeds were in common use, and would be found in every house. They probably were brought from the region of Jericho or from the banks of the Jordan. Reeds were used to make fences, mats, canopies on the terraces, shelters against the sun. A reed was placed in Jesus' hand in imitation of the long scepter, the emblem of power. And some hours later, a reed was used to extend to Jesus a sponge which had been soaked in vinegar (Matt. 27:48) or rather in the beverage which was prepared for those being executed in order to alleviate their suffering somewhat.

108.   A branch of ratab.

❷ According to the first two Evangelists, the condemnation was followed by a scourging. In Luke, however, the scourging precedes the condemnation; the implication is that Pilate thought that this would perhaps avoid capital punishment. In John, it is inserted in the middle of the interrogation, thus before the judgment has been rendered. In any event, the scourging was a regular measure and not at all whimsical. In other words, it was not like the things that happened on the initiative of the soldiers — which, incidentally, are not fully understood by scholars: were they simply acts

124

1 *They came to a place called Golgotha (which means the place of a skull) (Matthew 27:33; Mark 15:22; Luke 23:33; John 19:17)*

of bullying, or the jesting of the palace guard, or carnivalesque games, or saturnalia? Pilate had Jesus scourged, but he would not have had this right with an accused person who was also a Roman citizen, as was the case a few years later with the apostle Paul (Acts 22:24–25).

109. Jerusalem with its walls.

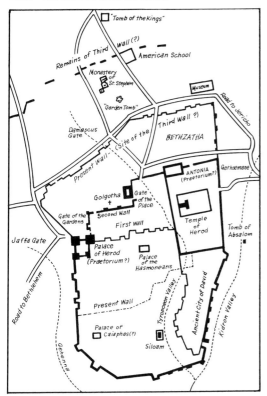

1 Although Golgotha is almost 2500 feet above sea level, it is not the highest point in Jerusalem. Moreover, the Gospels never say that Golgotha was a hill. But there is an oriental custom of calling a region after a traditional or legendary word. Thus there was a place, near the gates of Jerusalem and outside the walls, called "the skull." What skull? We do not know. It is unlikely that it was called such because of the physical form of the place, since during Jesus' time there already was the custom of calling by the name *ras* ("head") certain natural outcroppings which had absolutely no similarity to a human shape. Rather, a much simpler explanation is possible. This region was the scene of burials (John 19:41), and a poorly sealed tomb, damaged by the action of dogs and jackals, could one day have given up a skull, whence the appellation "Golgotha."

Today the site is covered by a church, full of gilded objects and sacred reliefs. It is divided between the Greeks and the Latins. We should not be scandalized by the present situation: the secular conflicts, the pitched battles, and the sacristy quarrels of the Church of the Holy Sepulcher are living proof that He is not dead, since the fights are over who alone shall worship there.

125

1 *And as they led him away, they seized one Simon of Cyrene, who was coming in from the country, and laid on him the cross, to carry it behind Jesus (Luke 23:26; Matthew 27:32; Mark 15:21)*

2 *They offered him wine to drink, mingled with gall (Matthew 27:34; Mark 15:23)*

3 *They crucified him (Mark 15:24; Matthew 27:35; Luke 23:33; John 19:18)*

If, as we maintain, the praetorium was on the site of Herod's palace, the procession must have left Jerusalem by the Gate Gennath ("of the Gardens") and followed the city wall (on the right) to Golgotha. Nevertheless, a more important route should also be considered: this route would go through the city to another gate (called in successive periods, the Gate "of Ephraim," or "of the Yeshana," or "of the Place"). In both of these hypotheses, the place of crucifixion would be outside the city.

❶ Only the Synoptics speak of this incident. Mark adds a detail: Simon of Cyrene was the father of Alexander and Rufus. From the praetorium to the traditional site of Golgotha, the distance in a direct line (leaving from the Gate Gennath) is not far: about a quarter of a mile. However, it is possible that the condemned persons (now a total of three; cf. Matt. 27:38; Mark 15:27; Luke 23:32; John 19:18) were made to follow a longer route through the streets of the western part of the city. It was traditional that those who were to be executed were paraded before the population, so that the people would be properly warned. If this were the case, the route would be noticeably longer, to a minimum, perhaps, of 650 yards. It is easy to understand why Jesus, who had begun by carrying his own

instrument of execution (John 19:17), shortly afterward had to be relieved of it. There is nothing strange about finding there a man who was returning from the country, especially if the procession was already outside the city, and thus beyond the Gate of the Gardens. This is one more argument for claiming that it was not yet Passover, but only the "preparation" for it (thus Nisan 14); otherwise, the day would have been a holiday and all work would have ceased, in the city as well as in the country.

❷ Once arrived at the place of execution, and before being put on the cross, the condemned persons were offered a beverage which was meant to stupefy them: wine mixed with gall (Matthew) or with myrrh (Mark). This was done in accordance with the prescription of Proverbs 31:6–7. Jesus refused to drink what was presented to him, undoubtedly to show that he was not afraid of suffering and that he wanted to approach it with full consciousness.

❸ The Gospels have given us no details on the methods of this horrible form of execution, one of the cruelest which antiquity had invented. The cross was made of two pieces, one vertical, the other a shorter transverse. The transverse was attached either at the very top of the vertical

1 *Then they sat down and kept watch over him there (Matthew 27:36)*

2 *They divided his garments among them by casting lots (Matthew 27:35; Mark 15:24; Luke 23:34; John 19:23–24)*

or a little below the top. Was the cross put together in advance, or on the spot? It has often been believed that the condemned had to carry only the horizontal piece (*patibulum*) on his back; the vertical beam was left at the place of execution. As far as the wood of the cross is concerned, we must be content with being ignorant as to its type.

A mile or so west of Jerusalem the Monastery of the Holy Cross purports to commemorate the site where the tree grew which later was used for the cross. But this is only a pious legend.

The body could be tied or nailed to the cross. The latter was the case with Jesus (John 20:25). The agony of the suffering could last several hours. On this point, information differs: in Mark (15:25), the Crucifixion took place at 9 A.M., and death came at 3 P.M. (15:33). For John, on the contrary, they were still in the praetorium "about the sixth hour" (19:14), that is, about noon. In passing, we should point out that this would have given more time for the appearance before Pilate as well as for the deliberations of the Sanhedrin which preceded it. Once again, John seems to have been in possession of detailed information which gives to his testimony an unrivaled importance.

110.   The instruments of the Passion in a Maronite church.

❶   This is a marvel of observation. The soldiers in charge of guarding condemned persons and of being present at their slow death could not remain standing, even though they were Romans. They had adopted the custom of the country: squatting on their heels, they waited.

❷   It was the custom, if not the right, for the executioners to appropriate the clothing of the condemned person. In this case, there must have been a mantle, a tunic, a belt, and perhaps sandals. Again, John provides details that are missing in the Synoptics: there were four soldiers, and thus the division was made in four parts. But how could so few things be divided into four, especially if the

127

1 *And over his head they put the charge against him, which read, "This is Jesus the King of the Jews" (Matthew 27:37; Mark 15:26; Luke 23:38; John 19:19)*

2 *And those who passed by derided him (Matthew 27:39; Mark 15:29)*

tunic were to come out in one piece? Such a division could be made if we added something similar to the modern *keffiyeh*, which more or less takes the place of a head-covering. It is unlikely that Jesus was without some such headgear. How were the lots cast? This is not indicated, but two methods may be suggested. One would be by tossing a coin, which would have a different image on either side. The other method, which we would favor, would be simply that of casting dice. There is clear evidence of the existence of dice during this period.

❶ John, again, gives additional information: the inscription was in Hebrew, Latin, and Greek (19:20). These were the three languages of the time. Hebrew (in reality, Aramaic), was spoken by the majority of the population; Latin was the language of the occupiers; Greek was the language of commerce, of the cultivated people, but also of the Jews of the Diaspora (who were numerous in Jerusalem during the time of Passover). During the period of the British mandate, official texts were again written in three languages: Hebrew, English, and Arabic. The *titulus* over the cross was standard; it was meant to inform those who saw the execution of the reason for it.

❷ Passersby must certainly have been numerous. For one thing, there was a road near this region, leading from Jerusalem (via the Gate of the Place) to the countryside. Also, there are great numbers of the curious in the Orient. More than elsewhere, perhaps, the Orient has such people who pass the day literally "standing idle" (Matt. 20:3). Quite naturally, there were those who had been against Jesus from the very beginning: chief priests, scribes, elders. They had come for the finish, and were not to be outdone in insults and sarcasm. The two thieves also joined in (Matt. 27:44), until one of them thought better of it and, after having rebuked his comrade, engaged Jesus in the well-known dialogue (Luke 23:39–43).

111. Trilingual inscription at sea level.

1 *Now from the sixth hour there was darkness over all the land until the ninth hour (Matthew 27:45; Mark 15:33; Luke 23:44)*

2 *One of them . . . took a sponge, filled it with vinegar, and put it on a reed (Matthew 27:48; Mark 15:36; Luke 23:36; John 19:29)*

3 *The curtain of the temple was torn in two, from top to bottom (Matthew 27:51; Mark 15:38; Luke 23:45)*

4 *There were also many women there, looking on from afar (Matthew 27:55; Mark 15:40; Luke 23:49)*

❶ This reminds us of the Maundy Thursday in 1927 (April 15) which we spent at Jerusalem. After a morning of blue sky, the horizon rapidly darkened. Heavy and threatening clouds covered the city quite literally at the hour indicated in the Gospels: "from the sixth hour until the ninth hour." From noon to 3 P.M., it was almost as dark as night. This fit so perfectly with the Maundy Thursday services (of the Protestants in the Weisenhaus Chapel and of the Catholics in the Church of the Holy Sepulcher) that one could not read the sacred texts without a shiver. On this anniversary day, nature itself mourned, and this contrasted so strongly with the brilliant morning sun that many were deeply impressed. After almost forty years, we still feel it.

❷ This was done not to mock Jesus, but, on the contrary, to quench his thirst. It was a rather curious beverage, vinegar "cut" with water. It is mentioned in the meal which Boaz offered to his harvesters (Ruth 2:14).[1]

[1] In KJV but not in RSV. According to the Interpreter's Bible, this midday meal consisted of sour wine, vinegar, and parched grain.

❸ According to Josephus, two veils existed in the temple, one at the entrance and the other between the *hekal* and the *debir;* which veil is referred to here we have no way of telling. It is to this veil that the anonymous author of the Letter to the Hebrews alludes (10:20). In 1878, Clermont-Ganneau wondered if the veil, mentioned by Pausanius, in the temple of Zeus on Olympus (offered by Antiochus) could not have been that from the temple at Jerusalem (which was profaned and pillaged by the Seleucid king in 167 B.C.). This hypothesis has not been and could not be demonstrated, and no exegete seems to have accepted it.

❹ Once again, this is a precise touch. In the Orient, there is always a strict separation between women and men in assemblies. The women seem to have gathered immediately, apparently somewhat apart and withdrawn. The Synoptics note that, besides the soldiers, there were some anonymous persons ("those who passed by") near the cross, plus the chief priests, scribes, and elders. This was the group of men. A bit further off, the group of women: the Galileans, mentioned previously (Luke 8:3) and now once again present, faithful to the end.

1 *Standing by the cross of Jesus were his mother, and his mother's sister, Mary the wife of Clopas, and Mary Magdalene (John 19:25)*

2 *When it was evening, there came a rich man from Arimathea, named Joseph. . . . He went to Pilate and asked for the body of Jesus (Matthew 27:57–58; Mark 15:42–43; Luke 23:50–52; John 19:38)*

Some are designated by name: Mary Magdalene; Mary the mother of James the younger and of Joses; Salome (Mark 15:40), who could have been "the mother of the sons of Zebedee" (Matt. 27:56) — elsewhere it is attested that she had made the trip to Jerusalem (Matt. 20:20). But there were others as well, as may be concluded from the phrase "among whom" which preceded the designation.

❶ The Fourth Gospel provides further details in indicating that also present were Jesus' mother and "the disciple whom he loved," which is a habitual way of designating John. The text, however, gives rise to an obvious question: how many women are involved, three or four? Furthermore, is it possible to establish equivalences? Is Mary the wife of Clopas the same as Mary the mother of James and Joses? If there were four women, would not the sister of Jesus' mother be Salome the mother of the sons of Zebedee? There are many questions and even more answers. We think that the Johannine passage speaks of four women: Jesus' mother, Mary the wife of Clopas (the same as Mary the mother of James the younger and Joses), Mary Magdalene, and finally, the sister of Jesus' mother. The latter can be identified with no one except Salome, who would also have been the mother of the sons of Zebedee (who would therefore be Jesus' first cousins). This relationship does not seem to be irreconcilable with the vocation of James and John as it is reported to us (Matt. 4:21; Mark 1:19).

112. Women looking on from afar.

❷ A man, previously unknown, appears out of the shadows and, as soon as his gesture of humanity is accomplished, he returns there. All that we know of him is that he came from Arimathea (to be identified with Rentis, some 15 miles northwest of Ram Allah), that he was a member of the Sanhedrin, that he was a secret disciple of Jesus, and that he was wealthy. It took courage for him to compromise himself so quickly. His position permitted him to go to the procurator and obtain the body of one of the executed persons. It was late. The sun had not yet gone down, but it was necessary to hurry, for the sabbath was about to begin. Moreover, if the Johannine version is accepted, it was a particularly solemn sabbath (John 19:31), since it was also the first day of the Feast of the Passover. According to Jewish Law, no corpse could remain exposed on the sabbath. The legalism of some thus accorded with the humanity of others.

Jesus' body was brought down — he had been dead now for two hours—and wrapped in a shroud. From earliest antiquity, the ancients had the custom of protecting their dead with a mat, a skin, or a more or less precious cloth (according to the wealth of the deceased). Slight traces of white, fragments of brown, bits of crimson cloth — such are what we have gathered from the tombs that we have discovered. Instead of digging a grave, the Jews preferred to cut deep niches into the cliffs, which they then fixed up and decorated. Since it was necessary to protect the tomb against animals and birds, stones were heaped up in front of it, especially if the tomb was single. But in family tombs, where there were several niches with one entrance, the entrance was closed with a large, circular stone (in the form of a millstone). This stone could be rolled at will and slipped easily into a groove carefully hollowed out of the rock. This is certainly the type of stone that Joseph of Arimathea, with the aid of Nicodemus (mentioned only by John; cf. John 19:39–42), placed in front of the cave (Matt. 27:60; Mark 15:46). This cave-tomb had been prepared for Joseph, and no one had yet been buried there.

John gives a further, and very important, detail. The place of crucifixion and the place of burial were located in the same

113. The tomb of Jesus according to the data of the Gospels.

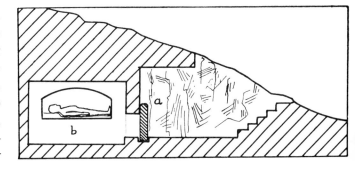

1 *Mary Magdalene and the other Mary were there, sitting opposite the sepulchre (Matthew 27:61). Mary Magdalene and Mary the mother of Joses saw where he was laid (Mark 15:47). The women . . . saw the tomb, and how his body was laid (Luke 23:55)*

2 *They went and made the sepulchre secure by sealing the stone and setting a guard (Matthew 27:66)*

area (19:41). The Church of the Holy Sepulcher, in its architectural complex, covers both places. But also, in one of the chapels of the church, one can see, even today, some Jewish tombs (of the *kokim* type) cut right into the rock. This proves that the area served as a cemetery during Jesus' day. This is a weighty argument, one not to be passed over in silence, when one defends the authenticity of the Holy Sepulcher — or rather, when one defends its location there, since nothing remains of the tomb of Jesus (nothing visible, at least) in this building which entirely covers it.

❶ These women were remarkably loyal; they remained there alone after night had fallen. They could not go away, for this would seem to them to be an abandonment on their part. This is a new and extraordinarily precise detail: the women were not seated on the tomb, but opposite it. The tomb, in fact, was cut into the rock and one had to enter it on a level.

❷ Some of the scribes and Pharisees, fearing that the disciples of Jesus would come and steal the body of their master in order to claim a miracle later, asked Pilate to provide a guard for the tomb. Soldiers were put at their disposition. This was the next day. As an additional precaution, the stone covering the tomb was sealed. This operation is simple, and we have often witnessed it; it requires only a little dirt mixed with chopped straw. The mud veneer dries quickly in the sun, and the sealing is immediately accomplished.

114. The Entombment. *Salers.*

VIII. Resurrection and Ascension

1 *Mary Magdalene, and Mary the mother of James, and Salome . . . very early on the first day of the week . . . went to the tomb when the sun had risen (Mark 16:1–2; Matthew 28:1; Luke 24:1; John 20:1)*

● The Evangelists differ on many points in their accounts of the Resurrection. But why wonder at this? The same event recounted by ten witnesses will be reported in ten different ways. All will be of good faith, each will be persuaded of the truth of his account, each will believe that he is right. Yet in all the accounts, one thing will be of importance. In the case of the Resurrection narratives, this important item is the following: Jesus had been placed in the tomb on Friday before nightfall; two days later, on the morning of the "first day of the week," the tomb was found empty.

All are agreed on one point: the discovery was made at a very early hour. Mark is the clearest on this: it was daybreak, just after the sun had risen. This is similar to what the Arabs mean by the phrase *Koullish nousse sebah* (there is a slight nuance in that this phrase refers to the moment immediately preceding sunrise, when the sun has not quite peeked over the horizon). It seems that it was this instant when the great day of Passover began. However, according to John it was still dark when Mary Magdalene arrived at the tomb. John does not give the names of the first witnesses, but from the other Gospels we learn that they were women only. This is infinite justice: those

who had been the last to leave the accursed place should be the first to discover the miracle. Besides Mary Magdalene, whom all accounts mention (truly, as a leader of the group), there was "the other Mary," that is to say certainly, Mary the mother of James and Joses (Matt. 28:1; Mark 16:1; Luke 24:10), Salome (Mark 16:1), and Joanna (Luke 24:10). The latter had been mentioned before (Luke 8:3) but had dropped out of view. Now she reappears, at least on this list of honor, for she was probably, if not certainly, in the anonymous group mentioned as "looking on from far off" on the afternoon of the Crucifixion.

The second fact is that the stone of the tomb had been rolled away (or was to be rolled away). We should not try to understand how or by whom. In the face of a miracle, all the ins and outs remain unexplained and inexplicable. Otherwise there would no longer be any miracle. What is certain is that the women who arrived at the tomb wondered who would roll away the stone for them (Mark 16:3). As we have pointed out, the tomb was of a type whose entrance was closed off by a millstone-shaped stone which one had to "roll" in order to displace it from its position. Two examples, at Jerusalem itself, illustrate

133

1 *They entered the tomb (Mark 16:5; Luke 24:2)*

2 *"They have taken the Lord out of the tomb, and we do not know where they have laid him" (John 20:2)*

115. A rollable stone. *Tomb of the Herods.*

this arrangement: the first is at the "Tomb of the Kings" (in reality, the tomb of the family of Helen of Adiabene), and the second is at the Tomb of the Herodian Family (presently in the Israeli zone, in the quarter of Nikephoria, west of the old city). Thus the description accords perfectly. And the stone had been rolled away. . . .

❶ It was therefore an important tomb, perhaps with a small vestibule opening on the sepulchral chamber. One could enter the tomb easily and stand upright inside it.

❷ This passage from John indicates the first impression of the women. They were thinking primarily of a transfer of the body rather than a violation of the tomb. Such violations are frequent, with the thieves thinking more of the precious funerary accoutrements than of the deceased themselves. On the other hand, the transfer of bodies was not uncommon, the purpose being to free certain sepulchers in order to assign them to other persons.

In this regard, we should mention the rescript of the emperor Augustus, which was inscribed on a stone found at or on the way from Nazareth.[1] This rescript states that anyone transporting a body from one tomb to another was liable to punishment by death. Certain scholars have even thought that the emperor Augustus mentioned in the rescript is Tiberius and that the latter was responding thus to a consultation with Pilate, following the "empty tomb" of Easter morning and a complaint registered by the Pharisees. If this had been confirmed, the stone of Nazareth would have been a capital document for the gospel history. Unfortunately, it appears that the emperor who promulgated the rescript was Augustus, who died in A.D. 14, thus well before the events in Jerusalem. Its importance, however, should not be minimized, for it shows at least that the disciples would have been risking their heads in taking the body of Jesus from the tomb of Joseph of Arimathea. Furthermore, in the state of discouragment in which they found themselves, they would have been quite incapable of this.

116. Rescript from Nazareth.

[1] A complete bibliography is found in our *Malédictions et violations de tombes* (Paris: Geuthner), p. 64, where we have given an overall view (pp. 64–76) of the theses proposed. The most important authors who have occupied themselves with the question are F. Cumont, in *Revue historique*, 163 (1930), pp. 241–66; Abel in *Revue biblique* (1930), pp. 567–71; M. Goguel, in *Revue d'histoire et de philosophie religieuses*, (1930), pp. 289–93; E. Cuq, in *Revue historique de droit français et étranger* (1930), pp. 385–410; (1932), pp. 109–26; J. Carcopino, in *Revue historique* 166 (1931), pp. 77–92. Carcopino has given the best interpretation of the document.

1 *Peter then came out with the other disciple, and they went toward the tomb. They both ran, but the other disciple outran Peter and reached the tomb first; and stooping to look in, he saw the linen cloths lying there (John 20:3–5)*

2 *Simon Peter . . . went into the tomb; he saw the linen cloths lying, and the napkin, which had been on his head, not lying with the linen cloths but rolled up in a place by itself (John 20:6–7)*

3 *That very day two of them were going to a village named Emmaus, about*

❶ According to Luke (24:12), only Peter went to confirm what the women had recounted. The Johannine account is much more alive and vibrant in recording this event. If Peter was outdistanced, it was because the younger John had better wind and more supple legs. What we want to emphasize here is the detail which John includes: *"stooping to look in, he saw. . . ."* Luke (24:12) has retained the same detail: *"stooping and looking in, he saw. . . ."* The explanation is simple: the door of the sepulcher is always lower than the line of vision of a man standing. In order to see what is going on inside, it is therefore necessary, if one does not enter, to stoop. This is what John, first, and then Peter did.

❷ Once again, John gives a very precise report of the state of things. The Evangelist has very carefully distinguished between the linen cloths which, dipped in aromatic oils, had been wrapped about the body of Jesus, and the napkin which had been wrapped around his head. This is undoubtedly a recollection of the concerted action of Joseph of Arimathea and Nicodemus (John 19:40). It should be recognized that this version is opposed to that of the Synoptics, according to which Joseph had time only to wrap Jesus in a linen shroud (Matt. 27:59; Mark 15:46; Luke 23:53), whereas it was left to the women to bring, on Sunday morning, the aromatics and other products with which to prepare the body (Mark 16:1; Luke 24:1). Thus, from the very first there were two traditions. If it were necessary for us to choose, we would prefer the Synoptic account. It is more plausible, given the haste that presided at the descent from the cross and then at the entombment at the close of day on Friday. They had been able to procure a shroud very quickly, but it was more difficult to acquire the aromatics, since all of Jerusalem was occupied much more with the sacrifice of the Passover lamb, which had to be finished before sundown.

❸ Of the different events which marked Easter Day, that which took place at Emmaus is one of the most impressive. It has inspired innumerable artists, who generally have depicted the moment of the breaking of the bread, which indeed constitutes one of the high points of the encounter between the two disciples and the unknown traveler.

Two Evangelists have reported the event for us. Mark gives a very brief account (16:12–13) and lays little stress on it; Luke,

seven miles from Jerusalem, and talking with each other about all these things that had happened (Luke 24:13–14)

fortunately, gives greater detail (24:13–35). On the morning of the Resurrection, two disciples (not any of the twelve) left Jerusalem to go to a village named Emmaus, about 60 stadia from the capital. On the way they talked about the tragedy which had just recently unfolded, during which Jesus had met his death. Suddenly a stranger approached and continued along with them. He seemed to be entirely unaware of the events that the two men recounted to him, including rumors to the effect that Jesus was alive, which seemed doubtful to them. The time passed, the day wore on, the journey continued. Finally the two pilgrims arrived at the village and invited their companion to share their meal. At the moment that the

stranger broke the bread, he was recognized, but vanished. The two rose and returned to the village, where they found the eleven.

The story is recounted with a dramatic simplicity, and one wonders where this village was that is thus immortalized. Contrary to what one might think, this identification is difficult and remains a point of controversy. According to the majority of manuscripts, the village was 60 stadia from Jerusalem, or about 7 miles. There is nothing at this distance, in any direction, which recalls the name; however, some scholars, considering the distance indicated, locate the village at el-Qubeibeh or at Quloniyeh.

117.   Village of Emmaus.

The Palestinian manuscripts, however, do not have 60 but 160 stadia, which would be about 20 miles. This time a possibility presents itself in the little village of Amwas (an Arab name which has conserved that of Emmaus), where an excavation carried on during 1924–25 uncovered ruins of a basilica dating from the 3rd century A.D. This basilica evidently was built to commemorate some great Christian recollection. There is no doubt that this recollection was that of the appearance of the Resurrected One, for Eusebius of Caesarea (3rd century A.D.) wrote: "Emmaus, where Cleopas came from, which is mentioned in Luke's Gospel, is now Nicopolis, an illustrious city of Palestine." Now, in the 1st century of our era, Emmaus was called Nicopolis, and this city was 20 miles from Jerusalem, that is, precisely 160 stadia.

Many objections have been raised against this localization. Is it possible for two men to have traveled 20 miles in the same day? Moreover, it is said, the return trip must have taken place, at least in great part, during the night, because when the travelers arrived at the village the day was already "far spent" (vs. 29). It is possible to explain this simply. At the time when they said that "the day is now far spent," there were still several hours of light remaining. The Old Testament provides proof of this. According to the account in Judges 19, the Levite went to Bethlehem to find his wife and was entreated by his father-in-law, with the same argument, to stay the night (vs. 9).

The Levite refused and started out on his way. There were two men, two asses, and a woman (in other words, according to custom, the woman went on foot). As they neared the heights of Jebus (Jerusalem), the servant wanted to halt the caravan, for "the day was far spent" (vs. 11). Nevertheless, they continued and it is indicated that the sun went down (vs. 14) when they were near Gibeah (modern Tell el-Ful). In short, between the two times, when "the day was far spent" and sundown, they had traveled about 9 miles!

As far as the possibilities of such a journey are concerned, they were considerable. According to Acts 23:23–32, several hundred soldiers left Jerusalem at 9 P.M. and returned the next morning after having traveled about 75 miles. A personal recollection: in Mesopotamia, on January 23, 1931, one of our workers set out at 10 A.M. and returned at 6 P.M., after having traveled alone and on foot some 30 miles.

1 *Then he led them out as far as Bethany, and lifting up his hands he blessed them. While he blessed them, he parted from them and was carried up into heaven (Luke 24:50–51, with variant reading)*

Thus, in our view, the location of Emmaus is confirmed. Thirty years ago it was nothing more than a small village, with low houses and winding little streets. The Judean hills, as Saint Jerome pointed out, are nearby, criss-crossed by footpaths. Everywhere the rocks are covered with field flowers. There is little vegetation — some thickets of holm oaks, from time to time clusters of olive trees. On Nisan 15, everything must have been covered with red anemones and pink cyclamens. On the western side one could sense the sea, with the well-known luminosity of maritime plains.

❶ This account confirms that of the same author in Acts 1:9–11. Tradition locates the event on the Mount of Olives. In the 4th century A.D., a woman by the name of Poemenia had a church erected there. The church was built on an octagonal plan, with a rotunda supported by columns and open toward the sky. In its center a small kiosk guarded, we are told, the imprint of Jesus' foot. In the 12th century it was restored by the Crusaders, then occupied by the Muslims, ruined, and is today nothing more than a small mosque. Christians may worship there on certain days, and entrance

118. Mosque of the Ascension.

is permitted to all of the caravans of tourists which are conducted to the Mount of Olives. We must make a confession: despite having lived in Jerusalem for two years and in spite of half a dozen return visits to the Holy City, we have never been able to make up our mind to enter the place. The

119. Relief of the Ascension. *Arles, Cloister of St. Trophime.*

memory of the Ascension directs our attention to heaven and not to a monument. However well-intentioned, such a monument succeeds only in obscuring that which it tries to recapture.

Once more, as too often in Palestine, where the hand of man has added to that of God, one can almost hear the voice of the angel to the women on Easter morning: *"Why do you seek the living among the dead? He is not here"* (Luke 24:5; Matt. 28:6). Rather, for those who have been able to see, he is on the shores of the Sea of Galilee, or at some bend of the Jordan, or on some rocky hillside of Judea. But even more, he is in his words, which have "the promises of eternal life," as two thousand years of life have already demonstrated. Heaven and earth will pass away, Palestine will undergo new metamorphoses, but the words — they will not pass away.

Synoptic Tables

— Herodian Dynasty

— Administration of Palestine
   During the New Testament Period

— Chronology of the Passion

TABLE I

HERODIAN DYNASTY

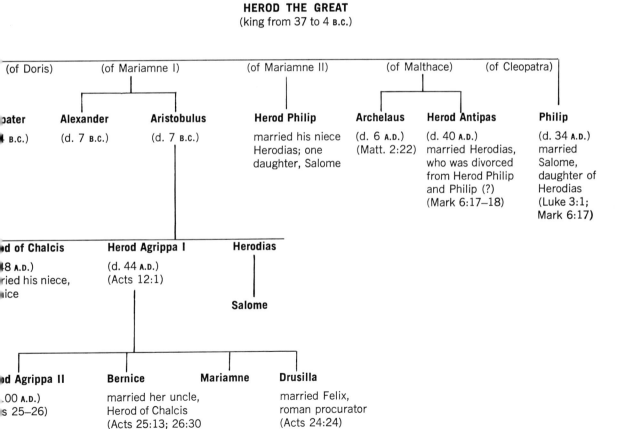

HEROD THE GREAT
(king from 37 to 4 B.C.)

(of Doris)	(of Mariamne I)		(of Mariamne II)	(of Malthace)		(of Cleopatra)
ᴅater	**Alexander**	**Aristobulus**	**Herod Philip**	**Archelaus**	**Herod Antipas**	**Philip**
ᴕ B.C.)	(d. 7 B.C.)	(d. 7 B.C.)	married his niece Herodias; one daughter, Salome	(d. 6 A.D.) (Matt. 2:22)	(d. 40 A.D.) married Herodias, who was divorced from Herod Philip and Philip (?) (Mark 6:17–18)	(d. 34 A.D.) married Salome, daughter of Herodias (Luke 3:1; Mark 6:17)

ᴅd of Chalcis	**Herod Agrippa I**	**Herodias**
ᴉ8 A.D.) ᴙried his niece, ᴉice	(d. 44 A.D.) (Acts 12:1)	
		Salome

ᴅd Agrippa II	**Bernice**	**Mariamne**	**Drusilla**
ᴕ00 A.D.) ᴕ 25–26)	married her uncle, Herod of Chalcis (Acts 25:13; 26:30 —widow at this time)		married Felix, roman procurator (Acts 24:24)

143

TABLE II
ADMINISTRATION OF PALESTINE DURING THE NEW TESTAMENT PERIOD

JUDEA SAMARIA IDUMEA	GALILEE PEREA	BATANEA TRACHONITIS GALANITIS ITUREA
4 B.C. to 7 A.D.	**4 B.C. to 39 A.D.**	**4 B.C. to 34 A.D.**
Archelaus, ethnarch	**Herod Antipas,** tetrarch	**Philip,** tetrarch
6 to 41: procurators Coponius Marcus Ambibulus Annius Rufus Valerius Gratus		**34 to 37:** Incorporated into the Roman province of Syria
Pontius Pilate (26 to 36) Marcellus Marullus	Death of Jesus, Easter, 28	
41 to 44: Agrippa I, king (Acts 12:1)	**30 to 44: Agrippa I,** king	**37 to 44: Agrippa I,** king
44 to 66: procurators Cuspius Fadus Tiberius Alexander Ventidius Cumanus Antonius Felix (Acts 23:24) Porcius Festus (Acts 24:27) Albinus Gessius Florus	**44 to 66: procurators**	**44 to 53:** Incorporated into the Roman province **53 to 100: Agrippa II,** (Acts 25–26)

144

TABLE III
CHRONOLOGY OF THE PASSION

SYNOPTICS				FOURTH GOSPEL		
Wednesday 6 P.M. to Thursday 6 P.M.	Nisan 14	preparation of the Passover sacrifice of the lamb unleavened bread, etc.		Wednesday 6 P.M. to Thursday 6 P.M.	Nisan 13	
Thursday 6 P.M. to Friday 6 P.M.	Nisan 15	Passover-Last Supper arrest trial crucifixion entombment		Thursday 6 P.M. to Friday 6 P.M.	Nisan 14	foot-washing arrest trial crucifixion entombment
Friday 6 P.M. to Saturday 6 P.M.	Nisan 16			Friday 6 P.M. to Saturday 6 P.M.	Nisan 15	Passover
Sunday		resurrection		Sunday		resurrection

Note: 6 P.M. = sunset

Selected Bibliography

A bibliography, even abridged, of works dealing with Palestine at the time of Jesus would require a list which by itself would have the dimensions of this work. Such a list cannot be given here. The titles included below are works which either have been useful in our study or are representative of certain historical and critical positions. We are far from sharing the perspectives of some of these works, but any objective study should mention them.

[Some of the following titles represent English translations of works listed in the original bibliography. In addition, an attempt has been made to provide a list of selected English-language works on special topics dealt with by the author.]

Translations and Commentaries

New English Bible; New Testament. Oxford and Cambridge University Presses, 1961.

The Holy Bible, Revised Standard Version. New York: Thomas Nelson and Sons, 1952.

BROWN, RAYMOND. *The Gospel According to John,* Vol. I (I–XII). "The Anchor Bible." Vol. XXIX. Garden City: Doubleday and Company, 1966.

GOGUEL, M. *Bible du Centenaire. Le Nouveau Testament.* 1928.

LAGRANGE, F. M. J. *Evangile selon saint Matthieu.* 3rd ed. 1927.

——. *Gospel of Saint Mark.* London: Burns, Oates and Washbourne, Ltd., 1930.

——. *Evangile selon saint Luc.* 1921.

——. *Evangile selon saint Jean.* 8th ed. Paris: Gabalda, 1948.

[An abridgment of Father Lagrange's studies on the Four Gospels was published under the title *The Gospel of Jesus Christ.* Trans. Luke Walker and Reginald Ginns. 2 vols. London: Burns, Oates and Washbourne, Ltd., 1938 (reprinted in 1 vol., 1947), and Westminster, Md.: The Newman Press, 1951.]

Atlases and Albums

AVI-YONAH, M., *et al. Views of the Biblical World,* Vol. V, *The New Testament.* Trans. Merton Dagut. New York and London: McGraw-Hill, 1961.

WRIGHT, G.-E., and FILSON, F. V. *The Westminster Historical Atlas to the Bible.* Rev. ed. Philadelphia: The Westminster Press, 1956.

Other Works

ABEL, F. M. *Géographie de la Palestine.* 2 vols. Paris, 1933 and 1938.

——. *Histoire de la Palestine.* Vol. I. 1952.

AHARONI, Y. *The Land of the Bible: A Historical Geography.* Trans. A. F. Rainey. Philadelphia: The Westminster Press, 1967.

ALT, A. *Where Jesus Worked: Towns and Villages of Galilee Studied with the Help of Local History.* Trans. Kenneth Grayston. London: The Epworth Press, 1961.

ARON, ROBERT. *Jesus of Nazareth: The Hidden Years.* Trans. Frances Frenaye. New York: Morrow, 1962.

BALY, D. *Geographical Companion to the Bible.* New York: McGraw-Hill, and London: Lutterworth Press, 1963.

——. *The Geography of the Bible.* New York: Harper, and London: Lutterworth Press, 1957.

BANKS, F. A. *Coins of Bible Days.* New York: The Macmillan Company, 1955.

BLAIKLOCK, E. M. *Cities of the New Testament.* London: Pickering and Inglis, Ltd., 1965.

BLINZLER, J. *The Trial of Jesus.* Trans. Isabel and Florence McHugh. Westminster, Md.: The Newman Press, 1959.

BODENHEIMER, F. S. *Animal and Man in Bible Lands.* Leiden: E. J. Brill, 1960.

BOUQUET, A. C. *Everyday Life in New Testament Times.* New York: Charles Scribner's Sons, 1954; and London: B. T. Batsford, Ltd., 1953.

BOVET, F. *Voyage en Terre-Sainte.* 1861. (In order to note better the changes that have taken place in Palestine during the passage of a century.)

BROWN, RAYMOND. *New Testament Essays.* Milwaukee: Bruce Publishing Company, and London: Geoffrey Chapman, Ltd., 1966.

COUCHOUD, P.-L. *Le mystère de Jésus.* 1924.

DALMAN, G. *Sacred Ways and Sites.* Trans. Paul P. Levertoff. New York: The Macmillan Company, and London: S.P.C.K., 1935.

DANIEL-ROPS, H. *Jesus and His Times.* Trans. Ruby Millar. 2nd ed. New York: E. P. Dutton and Company, 1956.

——. *Daily Life in Palestine at the Time of Christ.* Trans. Patrick O'Brian. London: George Weidenfeld and Nicolson, Ltd., 1962.

DUSSAUD. *Les decouvertes de Ras Shamra (Ugarit) et l'Ancien Testament.* 2nd ed. 1941.

FILSON, F. V. *A New Testament History.* Philadelphia: The Westminster Press, 1964; and London: SCM Press, 1965.

FINEGAN, J. *Light from the Ancient Past.* 2nd ed. Princeton: Princeton University Press, 1959; and London: Oxford University Press, 1960.

GOGUEL, M. *Jésus de Nazareth; Mythe ou Histoire?* 1925.

_____. *Life of Jesus.* Trans. Olive Wyon. New York: Harper Torchbooks, 1960.

GUIGNEBERT, CH. *Jesus.* Trans. S. H. Hooke. New York: Alfred A. Knopf, Inc., 1935.

JAUBERT, A. *The Date of the Last Supper.* Trans. Isaac Rafferty. Staten Island, N.Y.: Alba House, 1965.

JEREMIAS, J. *The Parables of Jesus.* Trans. S. H. Hooke. Rev. ed. New York: Scribner's, and London: SCM Press, 1963.

JOSEPHUS, FLAVIUS. *Works.* Trans. H. St. J. Thackeray, *et al.* (Loeb Classical Library.) 9 vols. London: William Heinemann, and Cambridge, Mass.: Harvard University Press, 1926–65.

KOPP, C. *The Holy Places of the Gospels.* Trans. Ronald Wells. New York: Herder and Herder, and London: Thomas Nelson and Sons, Ltd., 1963.

LOISY, A. *Les évangiles synoptiques.* 2 vols. Ceffonds, 1907–8.

MØLLER-CHRISTENSEN, V., and K. E. JORDT JØRGENSEN. *Encyclopedia of Bible Creatures.* Trans. Arne Unhjem. Philadelphia: Fortress Press, 1965.

MONNIER, H. *La mission historique de Jésus.* 1914.

PARMELEE, A. *All the Birds of the Bible.* New York: Harper, 1959; and London: Lutterworth Press, 1960.

PARROT, ANDRÉ. *Golgotha and the Church of the Holy Sepulcher.* Trans. Edwin Hudson. New York: Philosophical Library, and London: SCM Press, 1957.

_____. *The Temple of Jerusalem.* Trans. B. E. Hooke. New York: Philosophical Library, and London: SCM Press, 1957.

PEROWNE, S. *The Later Herods.* London: Hodder and Stoughton, Ltd., 1958.

_____. *The Life and Times of Herod the Great.* London: Hodder and Stoughton, Ltd., 1956.

RENAN, E. *The Life of Jesus.* London, 1864 (with many later editions).

RICCIOTTI, G. *The History of Israel.* Vol. 2. Trans. Clement Della Penta and Richard T. A. Murphy. Milwaukee: Bruce Publishing Company, 1955.

RUCKSTUHL, E. *Chronology of the Last Days of Jesus*. Trans. Victor J. Drapela. New York: Desclee, 1965.

SIMON, M. *Jewish Sects at the Time of Jesus*. Trans. James H. Farley. Philadelphia: Fortress Press, 1967.

STAPFER, ED. *La Palestine au temps de Jésus*.

STAUFFER, E. *Jesus and His Story*. Trans. Richard and Clara Winston. New York: Alfred A. Knopf, Inc., 1960.

WALKER, W. *All the Plants of the Bible*. New York: Harper, 1957.

WRIGHT, G.-E., and D. N. FREEDMAN (eds.). *The Biblical Archaeologist Reader*. Garden City: Doubleday Anchor Books, 1961. [See especially H. G. May, "Synagogues in Palestine," pp. 229–50.]

List of Illustrations

1. Palestine in the time of Herod the Great. 1
2/3. The Wise Men. Virgin and Child. *Portal of Moissac.* 2
4. The Emperor Augustus. *Museum of the Louvre.* 3
5. Palestine in the time of Jesus. 4
6/7. Bethlehem: Cave dwellings. General view. 5
8. Bethlehem. Basilica of the Nativity, exterior. 6
9. Central nave and iconostasis. 6
10. The Emperor Tiberius. *Museum of the Louvre.* 7
11. John the Baptist. *Charterhouse of Pavia.* 9
12. In the wilderness. 10
13. Palestinian locusts. 11
14. A pair of sandals. 12
15. The Jordan in Upper Galilee. 13
16. Greek Orthodox women on the banks of the Jordan. 14
17. The Mountain of the Temptation—Jebel Qarantal. 15
18. The pinnacle of the temple. 16
19. Lion of Sheik Saad (Karnaim). 17
20. Tiberias. 18
21. Magdala—Mejdel. 19
22. General view of Nazareth. 19
23. Sea of Galilee (view from the north). 20
24. Plain of Gennesaret. 20
25. Region of the Sea of Galilee. 20
26. The Jordan River at the Bridge of Jacob's Daughters. 21
27. Fishing boats on the Sea of Galilee. .. 22
28. A restless Sea of Galilee. 23

29. The Apostles John and Peter. *Arles, Portal of St. Trophime.* 25
30. The Scroll of Isaiah, from Qumran... 26
31. A street in Nazareth. 27
32. Mountain of the Precipitation. 27
33. General view of Cana. 28
34. Capernaum. The ruins of the synagogue. 29
35. Colonnade of the synagogue. 29
36. Capernaum. The synagogue after the excavation. 30
37. Ornamentation of an entablature. 30
38. Palmyra. Relief of "The Banquet." .. 32
39. Bedouin meal. 32
40. "Old wineskins." 34
41. Tyre. 37
42. Karn Hattin. 37
43. The "salt of the earth." 38
44. Palestinian lamp. 39
45. Bedouin costume. 41
46. Woman carrying ratab. 42
47. Woman bundling straw. 43
48. Tomb in the rock. 45
49. Harvest ablaze in Samaria. 47
50. Plowman in Samaria. 48
51. Plowman and sower in Samaria. 49
52. Children piping and dancing. 50
53. Plaque from the collection of Clercq. 51
54. Net drawn up on the beach. 53
55. "The blind leading the blind." 55
56. Syrophoenician women from the sarcophagus of the mourners (Sidon). *Museum of Istanbul.* 56
57. Lake Huleh. 57
58. Map of the Decapolis. 58
59. Mt. Tabor. 59

151

60. A child fallen into the fire. 60
61. Young shepherd. 62
62. Funeral procession. 63
63. Scorpion. 64
64. Palestinian woman going to draw water. 66
65. Plain of Askar. 67
66. Gerizim and Jacob's well. 67
67. Mt. Gerizim. 68
68. The Church of the Well of the Samaritan Woman. 68
69. A man was going down from Jerusalem to Jericho. 69
70. The robbers' cave. 70
71. Denarius. 72
72. The Mount of Olives. 74
73. Region of Bethphage. 75
74. She-ass and foal. 76
75. General view of Jerusalem. 77
76. General view of Bethany. 78
77. Woman drawing water at Bethany. . . 79
78. Tower in a vineyard. 80
79. Lock from Sur Baher. 82
80. "Whitewashed tombs." 83
81. Tomb of the Judges. 84
82. Tombs reputed to be those of Absalom, Saint James, and Zechariah. 84
83. The Wailing Wall in Jerusalem. 85
84. The mantle. 87
85. Sun, moon, stars. 89
86. Woman grinding meal. 89
87. Sheep and goats at pasture. 90
88. Perfume vase and saucer. 91
89. Ruins of the Tower of Siloam. 93
90. Village of Siloam. 93
91. Pool of Siloam. 94

92. Unfinished house. 95
93. Herod's Temple, Jerusalem. 97
94. Stele of the Vultures. The net of Ningirsuk. 98
95. The Sheep Gate at Jerusalem. 99
96. Foot of Pompeia Lucilia. *Museum of the Louvre* 100
97. Gushing vases. *Museum of the Louvre.* 102
98. The "Good Shepherd." 103
99. Ossuary. 105
100. The Upper Room and David's Tomb. 110
101. Chalice of Antioch. 111
102. "Stairway of Maundy Thursday." . . . 114
103. Gethsemane and the Mount of Olives. 114
104. The Garden of Gethsemane. 115
105. An olive tree in Gethsemane. 116
106. "The house of Caiaphas." 117
107. Akeldama. 119
108. A branch of ratab. 124
109. Jerusalem with its walls. 125
110. The instruments of the Passion in a Maronite church. 127
111. Trilingual inscription at sea level. . . . 128
112. Women looking on from afar. 130
113. The tomb of Jesus according to the data of the Gospels. 131
114. The Entombment. *Salers.* 132
115. A rollable stone. *Tomb of the Herods.* 134
116. Rescript from Nazareth. 135
117. Village of Emmaus. 137
118. Mosque of the Ascension. 139
119. Relief of the Ascension. *Arles, Cloister of St. Trophime.* 140
120. Tetramorph. *Chartres.* 166

Index of Scripture References

Genesis	
8:22	98
18:1 ff.	112
18:4	113
24:11	49, 66
26:1	95
31:39	104
35:19	1
41:57	95

Exodus	
5:7	43
12:6 ff.	107
13:1 ff.	82
13:11 ff.	82
20:14	40
20:17	94
21:17	55
21:23 ff.	40
22:13	104
22:27	48, 87
30:13	61
34:21	35

Leviticus	
11–15	83
11:7	46
12:3	6
12:8	6, 78
16:29	34

Numbers	
15:38 f.	82
21:9	99
34:11	21

Deuteronomy	
5:14	94
5:18	40
5:21	94
6:4 ff.	82
11:13 ff.	82

Joshua	
13:27	21
19:15 f.	1

Judges	
12:8	1
16:21	89
19:9	138
19:11	138
19:14	138

Ruth	
1:1	95
1:2	1
2:14	129

I Samuel	
16:1	1
17:34 f.	103–4
25:41	113

II Samuel	
21:1	95
24:18	85

I Kings	
4:25	98
18:2	95
18:43 ff.	60

II Kings	
1:2	52
4:38	95
17:6	65
17:24	65
17:25 f.	65

I Chronicles	
4:4	1
21:22	85
28:18	30

Nehemiah	
11:32	105

Psalms	
1:3	16
80:1	83
90:6	42
137:7 ff.	36

Proverbs	
31:6 f.	126

Isaiah	
8:6	94
13:13	86
21:11	54
24:17	98
24:19	86
40:3 ff.	8
45:9	119
46:1	83
52:7	92
58:11	102

Jeremiah	
2:13	87

Ezekiel	
27	56
27:36	56
32:3	98
38:20	86

Daniel	
9:27	86

Hosea	
7:12	98

Amos	
1:1	86
3:12	17, 104
6:4	33

Micah	
4:4	98
5:2	1

Habakkuk	
1:15	98

Zechariah	
3:10	98
9:9	76
14:5	86

I Maccabees	
4:36 ff.	104

153

II Maccabees

1:9	104
1:18	104
10:1 ff.	104

Matthew

2:1	1, 2
2:13	3
2:19	1
2:23	3
3:1	7, 11
3:3	8
3:4	11, 12
3:5 f.	12
3:7	12
3:11	13
3:13	13
4:1 f.	15
4:3	15
4:6	16
4:8	15
4:12 f.	19
4:18	22
4:21	130
4:23	31
5:1	38
5:13	38
5:14	38
5:15	38
5:18	39
5:25 f.	40
5:27	40
5:34 f.	82
5:39	40
6:9 ff.	92
6:16	34
6:19	41
6:25	41
6:27	41
6:28	42
6:30	42
7:3	83
7:3 ff.	43
7:6	43
7:9 f.	43
7:13	43
7:15 f.	44
7:19	44
7:24 ff.	44
8:11	113
8:14	31
8:16	31
8:23 ff.	22
8:28	23, 45
9:1	23
9:9	24, 29
9:10	33, 46
9:11	24
9:14	34
9:16 f.	35
9:20 ff.	47
9:23	46
9:27	47
9:35	44
9:37 f.	47
10:5	65
10:9	12
10:9 f.	48
10:12	49
10:14	50
10:27	50
10:29	92
10:42	49
11:8	50
11:16 f.	51
11:21 f.	56
11:23	31
11:30	51
12:1 ff.	35
12:15	31
12:24	52
12:43 ff.	51
13:3 ff.	52
13:18 ff.	52
13:24 ff.	52
13:31 f.	52
13:33	52
13:44	53
13:45 f.	53
13:47	53
13:54 ff.	26
13:55	25
13:57	26
14:3	53
14:3 ff.	18
14:6	53
14:12	18
14:13	23
14:15 ff.	54
14:17	43
14:22	23
14:25	54, 89
14:34	23, 54
15:2	55
15:4	55
15:14	55
15:21	18
15:21 ff.	55
15:22	56
15:24	65
15:39	23
16:2 f.	60
16:5	23
16:13 ff.	59
17:1 ff.	59
17:15	60, 61
17:24 ff.	61
18:6	61
18:10 ff.	61
18:12	62
18:23 ff.	62
19:1	64
19:24	43, 71, 83
20:1 ff.	71
20:2	81
20:3	128
20:6	71
20:8	71
20:11	72
20:12	72
20:17	75
20:20	63, 130
20:30	73
21:1	75
21:2	76
21:7	76
21:8	77
21:12	78
21:13	79
21:17	79
21:28	80
21:33 ff.	80
22:2 ff.	80
22:17 ff.	81
23:2	81
23:4	81
23:5	82
23:13	82
23:16	82
23:22	82
23:24	43, 71, 83
23:25	83
23:27	83
23:29	84
23:35	85
24:1 f.	85
24:3	86
24:15	86
24:16	87
24:17	87
24:18	87
24:20	88
24:26	88
24:28	88
24:29	88
24:40 f.	89
24:43	89
25:1 ff.	90
25:14 ff.	74
25:32 f.	90
25:35	90
26:3 f.	109
26:6 ff.	91
26:14 f.	109
26:17	106, 109
26:17 ff.	108
26:18	109
26:20	110
26:23	55, 111
26:26	111
26:26 f.	112
26:27	111
26:29	113

26:30	113	27:66	132	4:13 ff.	52	9:22	61	14:23	111
26:36	114	28:1	133	4:26 ff.	52	9:42	61	14:25	113
26:47	116	28:6	140	4:30 ff.	52	10:1	64	14:26	113
26:48	115			4:35	23	10:25	71	14:32	114
26:57	116	**Mark**		4:37 ff.	22	10:32	75	14:43	116
26:58	117			5:1	23	10:46	73	14:44	115
26:65 f.	121	1:3	8	5:1 f.	45	11:1	75	14:51 f.	115
27:1	118	1:4	11	5:13	46	11:2	76	14:53	116
27:2	119	1:6	11	5:21	23	11:7	76	14:54	117
27:3 ff.	118	1:7	13	5:22	46	11:8	77	14:64	121
27:7	118	1:9	7, 13	5:25 ff.	47	11:15	78	14:66	117
27:11 ff.	120	1:13	15, 17	6:3	25	11:16	91	14:72	118
27:15 ff.	122	1:14	19	6:6	44	11:17	79	15:1	118, 119
27:24	123	1:16	21, 22, 23	6:8	48	11:23	91	15:2 ff.	120
27:26	124	1:17	22	6:11	50	12:1 ff.	80	15:6 ff.	122
27:28	123	1:19	23, 130	6:17	53	12:14 ff.	81	15:15	124
27:29	123, 124	1:20	23	6:17 ff.	17	12:41 f.	91	15:17	123
27:30	124	1:21	29	6:21 ff.	18	13:1 f.	85	15:19	124
27:32	126	1:30	31	6:22	53	13:3	86	15:21	126
27:33	125	1:32	31	6:29	18	13:8	86	15:22	125
27:34	126	1:35	32	6:32	23	13:14	86	15:23	126
27:35	126, 127	1:38	32	6:35 ff.	54	13:15	87	15:24	126, 127
27:36	127	1:39	31	6:38	23	13:16	87	15:25	107, 127
27:37	128	2:4	33	6:45	23, 24	13:18	88	15:26	128
27:38	126	2:12	33	6:53	23	13:24 f.	88	15:27	126
27:39	128	2:14	24	7:3	55, 83	13:35	89	15:29	128
27:44	128	2:15	24, 33	7:5	55	14:1	109	15:33	127, 129
27:45	129	2:16	34	7:24 ff.	55	14:3 ff.	91	15:36	129
27:48	124, 129	2:18	34	7:26	56	14:12	106, 108, 109	15:38	129
27:51	129	2:21 f.	35	7:31	18, 57	14:13 f.	109	15:40	63, 129, 130
27:55	63, 129	2:23 ff.	35	8:10	23	14:15	110	15:40 f.	63
27:56	63, 130	3:6	35	8:13	23	14:16	108	15:42	107
27:57 f.	130	3:7	31	8:27	59	14:17 f.	110	15:42 f.	130
27:59	136	3:7 f.	36	9:2	60	14:20	55, 111	15:46	131, 136
27:60	131	3:13	38	9:2 ff.	59	14:22	111	15:47	132
27:61	132	3:22	52	9:18	61	14:22 f.	112	16:1	133, 136
27:62	107	4:3 ff.	52	9:20	61				

16:1 f.	133	5:19	33	9:10	23, 24	16:3	96	22:39	114, 116
16:3	133	5:24	33	9:12 ff.	54	16:19 ff.	96	22:47	115
16:5	134	5:27	24	9:28 ff.	59	17:2	61	22:54	116
16:12 f.	136	5:29	33	9:39	61	17:16	65	22:54 f.	117
		5:30	24	9:52 f.	65	18:9 ff.	97	22:61	117
		5:33	34	9:54 f.	65	18:11	97	22:66	118
Luke		5:36 ff.	35	9:62	48	18:12	34	22:71	121
		6:1 ff.	35	10:11	50	18:35	73, 96	23:1	119
2:1 f.	3	6:6	25	10:13 f.	31, 56	19:1 ff.	72	23:1 ff.	120
2:12	94	6:12	38	10:15	31	19:2	24, 72	23:6 ff.	122
2:16	94	6:17	31, 38	10:19	64	19:8	24	23:11	123
2:21 ff.	6	6:47 ff.	44	10:30	69	19:12 ff.	73	23:13 ff.	122
2:24	6, 78	7:2	29	10:33	65	19:14	73	23:22	124
2:39	6, 21	7:5	30	10:38 f.	104	19:27	73	23:26	126
2:41 ff.	6	7:11 ff.	62	10:38 ff.	92	19:29	75	23:32	126
2:44	7	7:14	62	11:2 ff.	92	19:30	76	23:33	125, 126
3:1 f.	7	7:25	50	11:12	43	19:35	76	23:34	127
3:3	11	7:36 ff.	92	11:24 ff.	51	19:41	77	23:36	129
3:4	8	7:37	63	11:26	63	19:45	78	23:38	128
3:7	12	7:44	113	12:6	92	20:9 ff.	80	23:39 ff.	128
3:19 f.	17	7:44 ff.	92	12:38	89	20:21 ff.	81	23:44	129
3:21	13	8:2	21	12:54	60	21:5 f.	85	23:45	129
4:2	15	8:2 f.	63	12:55	60	21:25	88	23:49	129
4:14	19	8:3	129, 133	13:1	93	21:29 f.	98	23:50 ff.	130
4:16 f.	25	8:5 ff.	52	13:4	93	21:34	98	23:53	136
4:21	27	8:11 ff.	52	13:6	98	22:1	109	23:54	107
4:25 ff.	28	8:19	31	13:15	94	22:7	106, 109	23:55	132
4:28 f.	25	8:22	23	13:21	52	22:8 f.	108	24:1	133, 136
4:29 f.	27	8:22 ff.	22	13:22	64	22:10 f.	109	24:2	134
4:31	29	8:26	23	13:29	113	22:12	110	24:5	140
4:38	31	8:30	63	13:32	71	22:13	108	24:10	63, 133
4:40	31	8:37	23	14:16 ff.	80	22:14	110	24:12	136
4:44	31	8:41	46	14:28 ff.	94	22:18	113	24:13 f.	136–37
5:1	21	8:43 ff.	47	15:3 ff.	61	22:19	111	24:13 ff.	137
5:4 ff.	22, 62	9:3	48	15:4	62	22:19 f.	112	24:29	138
5:5	23	9:5	50	15:8 f.	95	22:20	111	24:50 f.	139
5:7	23	9:9	63, 122	15:11 ff.	95	22:21	111		

John

1:23	8
1:28	12
1:43	24
1:46	26
2:1 ff.	28
2:6	29
2:12	19
2:14 ff.	78
2:19 f.	98
3:14	99
3:23	12
4:5 ff.	65–66
4:11	66
4:27	68
4:35	47, 99
4:43	19
5:2	99
6:1	21, 23, 101
6:5 ff.	54
6:23	101
6:59	29
7:2	101
7:10	102
7:35	102
7:37 f.	102
7:46	31
8:6	102
8:8	102
8:20	103
9:7	103
9:8	73
10	103
10:8	104
10:11	103
10:22	86
10:22 f.	104
10:40	104
11:1 ff.	104
11:6	104
11:18	79
12:1 ff.	91
12:13	77
12:20 f.	106
13:3 ff.	107, 113
18:1	114
18:2	116
18:3	116
18:12	8, 121
18:13	118
18:24	8, 118
18:28	107, 120, 121
18:28 ff.	120
18:29	121
18:31	121
18:33	121
18:38	121
19:1	124
19:1 ff.	122
19:2	123
19:4	121
19:7	121
19:9	121
19:12	121
19:13	121
19:14	127
19:17	125, 126
19:18	126
19:19	128
19:20	128
19:23 f.	127
19:25	130
19:29	129
19:31	131
19:38	130
19:39 ff.	131
19:40	136
19:41	125, 132
19:42	107
20:1	133
20:2	134
20:3 ff.	136
20:6 f.	136
20:19 ff.	112
20:25	127
21:1	21, 101
21:2 ff.	22

Acts

1:9 ff.	139
1:12	88
1:18 f.	119
4:6	8
5:36	104
5:37	104
8:9	3
10:2	106
13:6	3
13:16	106
13:51	50
18:3	25
22:24 f.	125
23:23 ff.	138

I Corinthians

11:23	108

II Corinthians

4:7	119

Hebrews

10:20	129

Index of Names and Subjects

A

Abd al-Malik, Mosque of   77
ABEL, F. M.   22, 120
Abila   58
Abila of Lysanias
  (Suk Wadi Barada)   8, 58
Abilene   8
Abraham   3, 96, 112
Absalom, tomb of   84, 114
Achaemenids   98
Acre   53
Adonis-Tammuz   6
adulterous woman   102
adultery   40
Aenon   12
Ahiram   83
Akeldama   118-19
Akiba   101
Aleppo   46
Alexander, son of
  Simon of Cyrene   126
Alexander the Great   55-56
Aliyan-Baal (see Baal-zebul)
Alphaeus, son of Zebida   30
Amman (see Philadelphia)
Amwas (see Emmaus)
Ananiah   105
Andrew   23, 25, 106
Annas   8, 118
anointing, the   91, 92
Anti-Lebanon   8, 22
Antioch, chalice of   112
Antioch of Pisidia   50, 112
Antiochus   129
Antiochus IV Epiphanes   86,
                           104

Antipater   1
Antonia, Tower of   120, 123
apostles   25
Archelaus   2, 3, 72, 73, 119
Arimathea (Rentis)   130
as   40, 48, 91, 92
Asclepius   100
Ashurbanipal   33
Asia Minor   96, 102
Askar (see Sychar)
ass   51, 61, 76, 94
Assumptionist Fathers   117
Assyrians   47, 65
Augustus Caesar   3, 8, 24, 59,
                       81, 134, 135
Auranitis   1
azymes
  (unleavened bread)   107

B

Baal-zebub   52
Baal-zebul (Aliyan-Baal)   52
Babylon   55
Badi-Lim   76
Balatah (see Shechem)
Balthasar   3
Banias (Paneas;
  see Caesarea Philippi)
baptism   12, 13-14, 17
Bar Cochba
  (see Simeon Ben Kosebah)
Barabbas   122
Bar-Jesus   3
Barnabas   50
Bartholomew   25
Bartimaeus   73, 96

Bashan, lion of   17
Batanea   1, 58
bed   33, 50
Bedouin   8, 41, 43, 44, 48, 49,
                       50, 62, 81, 109
Beirut   51
Beisan (see Beth-Shan)
Beit Lahm
  (see Bethlehem in Galilee)
belt   12, 48, 127
Belzetha (see Bethzatha)
bema   122
Benoit   80, 108, 120
Bethabara   12
Bethany (el-Azariyeh)   44,
            76, 79-80, 91, 92, 105
Bethany beyond the
  Jordan   12
Bethesda (see Bethzatha)
Bethlehem Ephrathah
  (in Judea) 1, 5, 6, 43, 94, 138
Bethlehem in Galilee
  (Beit Lahm)   1
Bethphage   75-76, 105
Bethsaida
  (Julias)   24, 31, 32, 54, 106
Beth-Shan (Scythopolis,
  Beisan)   17, 58
Bethzatha   100, 101
Bezatha (see Bethzatha)
Bezetha (see Bethzatha)
blind   47, 55, 73, 96
boat   22, 23, 53, 54
Boaz   129
Bozrah   8
bread   42, 43, 54, 89,
                       107, 109, 111

BULTMANN, Rudolph 102
burden 51, 81–82
BURROWS, Millar 102
Byblos 83

C

Caesarea by the Sea 50, 59
Caesarea Philippi
  (Paneas, Banias) 50, 59, 119
Caiaphas 8, 109, 116, 117,
  118, 120
Caligula 8, 86
Callirhoe 17
Cambyses 2
camel 32, 41, 43, 51, 71, 83
Cana
  (Kefr Kenna) 28, 29, 101
Canatha (el-Qanawat) 58
Capernaum (Tell Hum,
  Capharnaum) 21, 24, 25,
  29–31, 32, 33, 38, 61
Carmel 28, 53
Caspar 3
census 4–5, 104
centurion 29, 30
Chinnereth, Sea of
  (see Galilee, Sea of)
Chorazin
  (Kerazeh) 30, 31, 32, 81
Chuza 63
Cilicia 18
circumcision 6
Cleopas 138
Cleopatra of Jerusalem 8
Clercq, collection of 51

CLERMONT-GANNEAU, Ch. 129
Clopas 130
Coenaculum 110, 116
Constantine 6, 101
Constantinople 18
cross 63, 126–27, 129, 136
crown of thorns 123–24
crucifixion 107, 108, 122,
  126–27
Crusaders 18, 26, 66, 100, 139
cubit 41–42
cup 49, 83, 111–12
Cyprus 3, 96

D

DALMAN, G. 120
Damascus 18, 58
Damascus Gate 84
David 1, 103
David, Tomb of 110
David, Tower of 120
Dead Sea 17, 87, 91
Dead Sea Scrolls 11, 27, 62,
  82, 107
Decapolis 36, 45, 46,
  57–58, 106
Dedication,
  feast of the 86, 104
Deir el-Jenaineh 106
demons (unclean spirits)
  45–46, 51, 52, 63
denarius 48, 62, 70, 71,
  72, 81, 91, 92
Diaspora 3, 102, 106, 128
Didache 108

didrachma 61
Dion (Tell el-Ashari) 58
Dionysius Exiguus 1, 8
Dominus Flevit, Chapel of 77
drachma 61, 62, 73, 74, 95
DUSSAUD, R. 52

E

Eannatum 88, 98
earthquake 31, 86
Ecce Homo,
  Basilica of the 120
Ed-Damiyeh 64
Egypt 3, 102, 107
Egypt, the flight into 3
EISEN, J. A. 112
Ekron 52
El-Azariyeh (see Bethany)
El-Bireh 7
Eleazar 104, 105
Elijah 28, 60
Elisha 28
El-Qanawat (see Canatha)
El-Qubeibeh 137
Emesa 112
Emmaus (Nicopolis,
  Amwas) 136–39
Enlil 98
En-Nasirah (see Nazareth)
Ephraim, Gate of
  (see Yeshana, Gate of the)
Epiphanius 108
Epiphany 13, 14
Esdraelon, Plain of 21, 28,
  52, 61

Eshmun 56
Es-Salt 86
Essenes 15
Et-Tell 24
Et-Tur, Kefr 76
Etruria 113
Euphrates 9
Eurykleia 113
Eusebius 138
Exodus 107
Ezra 65

F

Fahil, Khirbet (*see* Pella)
field 35, 53, 65–66
fig trees 98
figs 41, 44
fire 42, 44, 60–61, 117
fish 23, 43, 53, 54, 62
fishing 22, 23
flood 44
flute player 46, 51
foot-washing 92, 107, 113
Fountain of the Virgin 28
fox 71
Franciscan fathers 29, 79–80

G

Gabbatha
(Lithostrotos) 122–23
Gadara (Umm Qeis) 45, 58
Galanitis 1
Galilee 1, 2, 8, 18, 21, 28, 31,
36, 44, 56, 57, 61, 63, 64, 92,
101, 106, 122

Galilee, Sea of 21–23, 36, 44,
45, 58, 62, 140
gall 126
Gallicante 113, 117
Gardens, Gate of the
(*see* Gennath, Gate)
garments 35
gate 43, 71
Gaul 2, 8
Gaumata, magus 2
Gaza 89
Ge-Hinnom (Gehenna) 118
Gemara 101
Gennath, Gate
(Gate of the Gardens) 126
Gennesaret 52, 54, 61
Gennesaret, Lake of
(*see* Galilee, Sea of)
Gerasa (Jerash) 45, 58
Gergesa (Kersa) 45, 46
Gerizim, Mount 44, 68, 82,
119
Gethsemane 107, 114, 116,
118, 121
Gezer 99
Gibeah (Tell el-Ful) 138
Gihon (Um ed-Daradj,
Virgin's Spring) 94, 103,
110
gnat 43, 71, 83
goats 41, 90
Golgotha 125, 126
Good Samaritan,
Parable of the 65, 69–70
Good Shepherd, the 103–4
grapes 44

grass of the field (*see* ratab)
Gratus, Valerius 118, 119
Greece 102
"Greeks" 102, 106
Gudea, Prince 99

H

Hadrian 6
Haifa 53
Hammurabi 40, 55
Hananel, Tower of 99
Hanukkah
(Festival of Lights) 104
Haram 16, 77, 86
harvest 35, 47, 52, 80,
94, 99, 101
Hasmoneans,
Palace of 118, 122
Hauran 8, 31, 61
Hazor 99
healing 47, 65, 73, 103
Hebron 11, 44, 82
Helen of Adiabene 134
Heracles-Melcarth 61
Hermon, Mount 8, 57, 59,
60, 61
Herod Agrippa II 120
Herod Antipas 2, 3, 8, 17, 18,
21, 24, 29, 36, 50, 54, 58, 63,
64, 71, 72, 101, 106, 122, 123
Herod, son of Mokimos 30
Herod the Great 1, 3, 4, 8, 17,
36, 53, 59, 72, 73, 77, 86, 99,
118, 120
Herodians 35

Herodias   17, 53–54
Herodotus   2
Herod's Gate
   (*see* Sheep Gate)
Hezekiah   103
Hillel   25
Hippos (Qalat el-Husn)   58
Holy Cross,
   Monastery of the   127
Holy Savior,
   Convent of the   116, 117
Holy Sepulcher   47, 86, 116,
                   125, 129, 132
honey   11
house   33, 41, 43, 44, 46, 50,
                   87, 88, 95, 117
Huleh, Lake   57

I

Idumea   2
Idumeans   1, 36
INGHOLT, Harald   25
Iran   2, 3
Iraq   49
Israel   7
Iturea   1, 8

J

Jacob's Daughters,
   Bridge of   22
Jacob's well   65–67, 101
Jaffa Gate   120
Jairus   46, 47
James the brother of Jesus   17

James (son of Alphaeus;
   James the younger)   25,
                        130, 133
James (son of Zebedee)   23,
                        25, 65, 130
Janneus, Alexander   101, 122
jar, water   29, 61
JAUBERT, A.   107
Jebel Druze   58
Jebel Qafzeh   28
Jebel Qarantal   15
Jebus (*see* Jerusalem)
Jehoshaphat, tomb of   84, 114
Jerash (*see* Gerasa)
Jeremiah   3
JEREMIAS, J.   120
Jericho   11, 12, 13, 15, 24,
      65, 69, 70, 72, 73, 88, 96, 124
Jeroboam   3
Jerusalem   3, 6, 11, 13, 18, 36,
      42, 51, 55, 60, 68, 69, 70, 71,
      75, 76, 77, 79, 84, 86, 87, 88,
      92, 97, 101, 102, 103, 104,
      106, 107, 110, 112, 118, 120,
      121, 122, 125, 126, 127, 128,
      129, 130, 133, 135, 136, 137,
                        138, 139
Jews   1, 32, 33, 34, 43, 46, 50,
      61, 65, 67, 81, 83, 86, 89, 95,
      102, 104, 106, 107, 118, 120,
         121, 122, 128, 131
Joanna   63, 133
Johanan   30
John (son of Zebedee) 23, 25,
                      65, 130, 136
John the Baptist 7, 8, 9, 11, 12,
      13, 15, 17, 18, 36, 54, 104

Jordan   58
Jordan River   1, 8, 12, 14, 16,
      21, 36, 45, 54, 57, 58, 59, 64,
         73, 104, 106, 124, 140
Joseph   3, 6, 7, 25
Joseph of Arimathea   130–31,
                        135, 136
Josephus   4, 5, 17, 25, 44,
      53, 60, 86, 99, 104, 119, 129
Joses   130, 133
Judas Iscariot   25, 109, 115,
                        116, 119
Judas Maccabeus   86, 104
Judas the Galilean   104
Judas the son of James
   (*see* Thaddaeus)
Judea   1, 2, 3, 11, 15, 25, 36,
      52, 62, 64, 72, 73, 81, 88, 92,
         103, 118, 119, 140
jug, water   49, 66, 109
Julia   91
Julias (*see* Bethsaida)
Julius Caesar   4
Justinian   6
Justos   30

K

Kalah (*see* Nimrud)
Karn Hattin   36
Kefr Birim   30, 44
Kefr Kenna (*see* Cana)
Kerazeh (*see* Chorazin)
Kerioth   25
Kersa (*see* Gergesa)
Khan Minyeh   29

Khan Oreimeh 21, 29
Khirbet Qumran 86
Kidron 44, 76, 79, 84, 104, 114, 118
kingdom of God 48, 71, 113
Kohl 29
Kouchakji brothers 112
Koziba 11

L

Lagash (Telloh) 38, 41, 88, 98
LAGRANGE, F. M. J. 108
lamp 39, 90
Larsa 53
Last Supper, the 107, 108, 110, 111
Lazarus 12, 79, 80, 104–6
Lebanon 57, 76, 96
Lebbaeus (see Thaddaeus)
Levi, son of Alphaeus (see also Matthew) 24, 33
Lights, Festival of (see Hanukkah)
lilies of the field 42
Lithostrotos (see Gabbatha)
locusts 11
LOFTUS, W.-K. 33
log 43, 83
Lord's Prayer, the 38, 98
Lord's Supper, the 107, 108, 110, 111, 112, 113
Lusignan, Guy de 36
Lydda 86
Lysanias 8

M

Machaerus 17, 18, 50, 104
Magdala (Mejdel) 21, 32, 63
magi 2–3
Maimonides 101
Malthace 8
manger 94
mantle 41, 47, 48, 73, 87, 127
Mar Sabas 11
Marduk 10
Mari 38, 40, 47, 53, 76, 96
Mark 115–16
Martha of Bethany 92, 96, 104, 105, 106
Mary Magdalene 21, 63, 130, 132, 133
Mary, mother of James the younger and Joses 130, 132, 133
Mary, mother of Jesus 6, 7, 130
Mary of Bethany 91, 92, 96, 104, 105, 106
Mary, wife of Clopas 130
Matthew (see also Levi, son of Alphaeus) 24, 25, 33
Massorah 101
Mauristan Argoun 46
Medes 2
Mejdel (see Magdala)
Melchart 56
Melchior 3
merchants in the temple 78–79, 101
merkaba 30
Meron 30

Mesopotamia 9, 42, 97, 138
mill 89
Millicent, Queen 79
millstone 61
mina (see Pounds, Parable of the)
Mishnah 46, 101
Moab, mountains of 16, 28
Moissac 96
Mokimos 30
moon 54, 88
Moses 16, 99, 102, 104, 119
Moses' seat 81
moth 41
multiplication of the loaves 54
Murabbaat 82, 87
Muslim 31, 43, 83, 139
Myriam 105

N

Nablus 86
Nabu 10
Nain (Nein) 62
Nannar (Sin) 54
navigation 22–23
Nazareth (en-Nasirah) 3, 6, 21, 25–28, 29, 62, 135
Nebi-Sahin 28
Nebo, Mount 16
Nein (see Nain)
net, fishing 23, 53
Nicodemus 101, 131, 136
Nicopolis (see Emmaus)
night 54, 89

Nikephoria 134
Nile 3
Nimrud (Kalah) 65
Nineveh 33
Ningirsuk 98

O

Olives, Mount of 76, 77, 79, 86, 91, 92, 105, 113, 114, 116, 139
Omar, Mosque of 77
Omayyads, Mosque of the 18
Onias III 3
ORFALI 29
Origen 12
Ornan the Jebusite, threshing-floor of 85
Osiris 90
oven 32, 42
ox 94

P

Palace of Herod the Great 120, 121, 122, 123, 126
Palestine 10, 15, 17, 18, 35, 42, 44, 47, 50, 52, 60, 65, 71, 76, 86, 91, 92, 98, 103, 112, 116, 119, 138, 140
Palmyra 24, 33
Pan 59
Paneas (Banias; see Caesarea Philippi)
paralytic 33, 44

Passover 7, 106–9, 110, 111, 113, 120, 121, 122, 126, 128, 131, 133, 136
Pater, Church of the 86, 92
Paul 25, 50, 125
Pausanius 129
pearls 53
Pella (Khirbet Fahil) 58
Pentecost 110
Perea 1, 2, 8, 17, 36, 64, 71, 72, 104, 105
Persians 2
Peter (see also Simon Peter) 59, 61, 117, 136
Pharisees 34, 35, 55, 71, 81, 82, 83, 84, 97, 122, 132, 135
Pharisee and the Publican, Parable of the 97
Philadelphia (Amman) 58
Philip 24, 25, 106
Philip, son of Herod 2, 8, 17, 24, 29, 50, 53, 54, 58, 59, 106
Philistines 89
Phoenicia 18, 28, 96, 102
Phoenicians 83
phylacteries 82
Pilate, Pontius 8, 50, 72, 93, 107, 108, 118, 119–20, 121, 122, 123, 124, 125, 127, 132, 135
Place, Gate of the (see Yeshana, Gate of the)
plow 48
Poemenia 139
Pompeia Lucilia 100
Pompeii 43

Pompey 58
pool 94, 100–1, 103, 110
Pounds, Parable of the 73, 74
praetorium 120, 121, 122, 123, 124, 126, 127
Precipitation, the 27–28
Presentation 6
prison 40
Prodigal Son, Parable of the 95–96
Ptolemy 15
publican (tax collector) 24, 33, 72, 97

Q

Qalat el-Husn (see Hippos)
Qasr el-Yehud 13
Quirinius, Publius Sulpicius 4–5, 104
Quloniyeh 137
Qumran 15, 27, 53, 62, 82, 99, 107

R

rain 44, 50, 60, 88
Ram Allah 130
Raphana 58
Ras Shamra 52
ratab 42, 123–24
Red Sea 53
reed 50, 124
refrigerium 97
Rentis (see Arimathea)
Resurrection 112, 133, 137

Rich Man and Lazarus,
    Parable of the   96–97
Riha   112
robbers   41, 69–70
rock, house built on the   44
Rome   73, 102, 119
roof   33, 43, 50, 87
Rufus   126
rust   41

S

sabbath   25, 32, 35, 44,
                    88, 107, 131
sacrifice   6, 78, 107, 109,
                        121, 136
Sadducees   34
Safaad (see Sepheth)
St. Anne's Church   100
St. Bertrand de Comminges 8
St. James, tomb of   84, 114
St. Jerome   139
St. Paul   108
St. Trophime   96
Sainte-Sion, Basilica of   110
Saladin   36
Salim   12
Salome, daughter of
    Herodias   53–54
Salome, mother of the
    sons of Zebedee   130, 133
salt of the earth   38
Samaria   1, 2, 3, 18, 21, 28, 47,
                64, 65, 73, 101
Samaritan woman at
    Jacob's well, the   65, 66–68

Samaritans   33, 65, 68, 69–70,
                               119
Samson   89
sandals   13, 48, 50, 113, 127
Sanhedrin   101, 107, 108, 109,
    116, 118, 120, 121, 127, 130
Sarandarion   16
Sargon   65
Satan   15
Saturninus, Sentius   4
Saul   103
"scepter"   124
scorpion   43, 64
scourging   124–25
scribes   34, 35, 81, 82, 84, 109,
            116, 128, 129, 132
Scythopolis (see Beth-Shan)
seed   52
Semakh   22
Semites   54
Sepheth (Safaad)   38
sepulchers (see also
    tombs)   18, 45, 134, 136
Serapis   100
Sermon on the Mount   36–38
serpents (see also vipers)   43,
                            64, 99
Severans   30
Shammai   26
Sharon, Plain of   61
Shechem (Balatah)   65, 66
sheep   41, 44, 61–62, 90,
                99, 100, 103–4
Sheep Gate
    (Herod's Gate)   99–100
Sheik Saad, lion of   17

shekel   48, 53, 61, 109
Sidon   18, 31, 36, 56,
                    57, 58, 65, 96
Siloam   44, 73, 94, 103, 110
Simeon Ben Kosebah
    (Bar Cochba)   87
Simon Macchabeus   15
Simon of Cyrene   126
Simon Peter
    (see also Peter)   23, 25, 33
Simon the Leper   91
Simon the Magus   3
Simon the Pharisee   92
Simon the Zealot   25
Sin (see Nannar)
Sinai   60
sinner(s)   24, 33, 63, 92
sky   60, 88
Smerdis   2
snare   98
Solomon   98
sower   48, 52
staff   48–49
star(s)   3, 88
stater   61
straw   33, 43, 132
Stuma   112
Suk Wadi Barada
    (see Abila of Lysanias)
sukkoth   101
Sumer   88, 98, 99
Sumerians   52, 54
summer   50, 98
sun   88
sundown   31–32, 54, 71, 72,
    87, 89, 107, 109, 121, 136, 138
sunrise   32, 54, 71, 72, 89, 133

Sur Baher 82
Susanna 63
swine 43, 46, 95–96
sycamore 73
Sychar (Askar) 66
synagogue 21, 25, 26–27, 29–30, 31, 44, 46, 47, 81
Syria 4, 8, 10, 11, 44, 47, 76, 86

T

Ta‘amireh 11, 62
Tabernacles, Feast of 101, 102
table 110, 112
Tabor, Mount 59, 62
Talents, Parables of the 62, 74–75
Talmud 25
Tammuz (see Adonis-Tammuz)
Tares, Parable of the 52
tax collector (see publican)
Tell el-Ashari (see Dion)
Tell el-Ful (see Gibeah)
Tell el-Husn 58
Tell Hum (see Capernaum)
Telloh (see Lagash)
temple 6, 15, 16–17, 36, 42, 59, 68, 77, 78, 79, 82, 84, 85, 86, 91, 97, 98, 99, 101, 103, 104, 107, 118, 120, 122, 129
Temptation 15–17
Thaddaeus (Lebbaeus; Judas the son of James) 25
Theophilus 7
Theudas 104

thief 41, 89, 134
thistles 44
Thomas 25
thorns 44, 52, 123
throne 83
Tiberias 21, 28, 50, 63, 101
Tiberias, Sea of (see Galilee, Sea of)
Tiberius Caesar 7, 21, 81, 119, 135
titulus 128
Tivoli 4
Tomb of the Herods 134
Tomb of the Judges 84
Tomb of the Kings 134
tombs (see also sepulchers) 18, 45, 46, 63, 79, 80, 83–84, 96, 106, 114, 118, 125, 131–32, 133–34, 135
tower 80, 93, 94
Trachonitis 1, 8
Transfiguration 59, 61
treasure 41, 53, 82
Tulul Abu el-Alayiq 72
tunic 12, 48, 55, 127, 128
Tyre 18, 28, 31, 36, 55–56, 57, 58, 61, 65, 96
Tyropoeon 110, 118

U

Ulysses 113
Um ed-Daradj (see Gihon)
Umm el-Amed 30
Umm Qeis (see Gadara)
Umma 88

unclean spirits (see demons)
Ur 52
Uriah 3

V

Varus, Q. 4
Vaux, Roland de 53, 86
veil of the temple 129
Vienne 2
Vincent, H. 100, 120
Vinci, Leonardo da 110
vinegar 124, 129
vineyard 71–72, 80, 94
vipers (see also serpents) 13, 17, 64
Virgin's Spring (see Gihon)
vultures 17, 88
Vultures, Stele of the 88, 98

W

Wadi el-Haram 36
Wadi Qelt 72
water 29, 41, 49, 61, 66–67, 79, 83, 89, 96, 101, 102, 110
Watzinger, C. 29
wedding at Cana 28–29
Wehrlin Collection 7
Weisenhaus Chapel 129
White Fathers 100
wilderness 8–11, 15, 16, 62, 88, 101
Wilson 29
wind 42, 44, 60
wine 29, 35, 69, 70, 112, 113, 126

wineskins	35	**Y**		**Z**		
winter	60, 87, 88, 98, 104, 117, 124	Yahweh	10, 65, 82, 83, 101	Zacchaeus	24, 72–73	
Wise and Foolish Maidens, Parable of	90	Yeshana, Gate of the (Gate of the Place, Gate of Ephraim)	126, 128	Zebedee	23, 63, 130	
				Zebida	30	
X		Yeshua ben Gilgola	87	Zebulun	1	
		yoke	48, 51	Zechariah	84, 85	
Xystus	118	Yudan, son of Ishmael	81	Zechariah, tomb of	84, 114	
				Zeus on Olympus	129	
				Zimri-Lim	76	

120. Tetramorph. *Chartres.*